I0007480

Fundamental C:
Getting Closer To The Machine

First Edition

Harry Fairhead

I/O Press
I Programmer Library

Harry Fairhead Fundamental C: Getting Closer To The Machine.
1st Edition
ISBN Paperback: 978-1871962604
First Printing, 2019
Revision 1

Published by IO Press   www.iopress.info
In association with I Programmer   www.i-programmer.info

Preface

C is a classic language and it is still an important language. This is because it is closer to the machine than other languages, but it still has enough abstraction for you to create programs that are more or less portable. Perhaps more important, it means you don't have to learn a new assembly language every time you switch hardware. So learn C and gain the advantage of its speed, simplicity and stay close to the metal. This approach is essential if you are going to create programs for the IoT or embedded processors, but it is also relevant to any program that makes direct use of hardware.

Most books on C treat it as if it was just a slightly different take on Java, or some other high-level language. C isn't Java with limited facilities. It is designed to do a very different job from most modern languages. The key to understanding C is not to just understand the language, what the specifications say, but how this relates to the hardware. C is only a logically constructed language when seen in terms of how it relates to the hardware.

For this reason it needs its own approach.

But what is that approach?

Low-level code works with the underlying representations of the data at the level of bits. In languages such as Java, Python and so on you don't often question how the data is stored or represented, but the creation of low-level C code does just this. You need to know about addresses, pointers and how things are represented using just binary. Dealing with such topics also brings us into contact with the scourge of the C world – undefined behavior. This cannot be ignored, as it is in so many other books on C, and here not only is it acknowledged, it is explained together with ways to avoid it.

C is a simple language and lends itself to being introduced in simple ways, but the simple constructs of C can be put together in ways that produce something complex or at least unexpected. I have tried to indicate how the simple parts of C are combined to make it more powerful than you might expect and how to avoid going too far and making it so obscure that it is difficult to understand.

In this book the emphasis is on standard C. If you want to know more about using C on POSIX-compliant and Linux-based systems, this is covered in its companion volume, ***Applying C For The IoT With Linux*** ISBN: 978-1871962611.

Harry Fairhead
March 2019

This book is a revised and updated version of the series of articles on the I Programmer website: **www.i-programmer.info**

To keep informed about forthcoming titles visit the I/O Press website: **www.iopress.info**. This is also where you will also find any errata and update information. You can also provide feedback to help improve future editions.

Table of Contents

Chapter 13   **219**
Files

Chapter 14   **233**
Compiling C – Preprocessor, Compiler, Linker

Chapter 1

About C

C is a good choice of language. It is still relevant because it is close to the hardware and no other language can take its place.

Why C?

C has a long history which I'm not going to bore you with, but it was invented in 1973 with the specific purpose of implementing Unix. Even today, it is the language that most operating systems are implemented in. It is also experiencing a resurgence because of its use in small Single Board Computers (SBCs) such as the Raspberry Pi, Arduino and other IoT devices.

The reason for its popularity in these areas is that the C language is modeled on what happens under the covers. Its facilities are close to what the machine actually does and it is fairly easy to follow how C is converted into assembly language for a particular machine.

Another way of saying this is that C is just one step of abstraction away from assembler, whereas other languages are trying to take as many steps of abstraction as possible from the underlying machine.

As a result it is reasonable, but not entirely accurate, to call C a machine-independent, high-level assembly language - but you can argue about such things to no real purpose or result.

The key point is that C is a lowish-level language and this makes it possible to write programs that are sensitive to the hardware available.

C programs can be compact, i.e. use little memory, and they can be fast. For operating systems and embedded hardware these are important considerations. C also makes it possible to deal directly with the hardware, something that is often impossible in other languages that explicitly set out to stop you doing this.

This brings us to the main disadvantage of C.

If it can be done, then it can be done in C, but not necessarily done well.

Another issue is that there are few safeguards in the C language and if you aren't careful, or if you actually want to, then bringing down the whole machine is possible. Not only can you crash the machine, but you can "brick" it - mainly by destroying the firmware or by disabling essential hardware. Don't get too worried, you have to try hard and know a lot before this is even a possibility.

What is more likely is that you can create a program that has inherent security problems. If this is an important consideration then you need to exercise caution when using C and one of the best ways of doing this is to use a good IDE, like NetBeans which will warn you when you use things that are inherently dangerous.

OK, so if C is such a good language, why not move to C++ which must be better still?

The idea that C++ is a better language than C is only partially true. C++ is a more sophisticated language. It is object-oriented and as such has to be a little slower than C, and its programs use slightly more memory. It is also arguable that C++ is not a good object-oriented language to learn. The reason is that its object-oriented features were added to C in a clever way, but over time the language has been repeatedly extended and today it is something of a mess that can confuse even the best programmer. While C++ is often the obvious choice for systems and utility programmers wanting to use object-oriented methods, it is probably not the best choice if you just want an object-oriented language. For example, the Linux kernel is still written in C, but many Linux applications are written in C++.

To be clear, C++ is still fast and it is still compact. Sometimes a C++ program can be as fast and as compact as the equivalent C program, but if you value efficiency above all else then C is still the best choice.

It is also the best choice for the complete beginner.

The reason is that it doesn't have the abstract sophistication of C++ and other object-oriented languages. It is a simple modular language which, as already mentioned, brings you into contact with underlying machine ideas. For a beginner wanting to master computing and computer science, this is really helpful.

When you are ready for the more advanced ideas that are certainly needed, you can move on to C++ and discover object-oriented programming, but don't be in too much of a hurry.

So C is a great first language for educational reasons and it is a practical and still important language.

What more could you want.

Standards and C

The first question facing the new C programmer is which dialect of C you are going to use. Unlike many other languages, the new versions of C haven't completely replaced older versions. This is because the simplicity of the C language is often the reason it it used. Later versions of C have tended to expand the scope of the language, which sometimes makes is unsuitable for its intended use. As a result, the most commonly used version of C, ANSI C, isn't the latest.

The earliest de facto standardized C was K&R, which was named after the book that introduced and documented it, **The C Programming Language** written by Kernighan and Ritchie in 1978. This dialect of C is no longer used.

The most important version of C is ANSI C, which was adopted as a standard in 1989 and is often called C89, or C90 to mark its adoption as an ISO standard as well. The terms ANSI C, ISO C, ANSI/ISO C, C89 and C90 are all used to refer to the same dialect of the C language.

After ANSI C the next standard was C99 in 1999. This is backward compatible with its predecessor and has one or two useful extensions, including some additional data types and in particular the ability to declare block-scoped variables, which make writing for loops easier. It also has IEEE 754 floating-point support in hardware, if available, and as a library if not.

If you can use C99 then it is a good choice with few drawbacks.

The most recent standard is C11, which was finalized in 2011. This introduces many changes that take C into more complex areas. For example, it has support for multi-threading in the language rather than just making use of whatever the operating system provides. There are many C programmers of the opinion that C11 is a C too far and prefer to stay with C99 or even ANSI C.

At the time of writing, C18 had been released, but this is mostly a "bug" fix to the C11 standard and adds no new language features. Work is currently underway on a new C standard, C2x, which promises backward compatibility, but little else is known at the moment.

The GCC compiler supports C89, C90 and C11 all at fairly complete levels of implementation.

You can spend a lot of time worrying about which version of C to use, but if you are writing code for embedded systems and the IoT, you have a lot more to worry about in variations in the libraries you will use and features that are missing due the hardware in use. From this point of view, the differences between C89, C99 and C11 are mostly minor.

In the most of this book we will use C99 simply because some of its extra features make life easier. However, the differences are minor and come down to the ability to use single-line comments and declare variables in for loops. No matter which C standard you decide to use, there will be times when you have to use facilities that are not provided by it but by libraries written in C. Once you go beyond the C standard the next best thing is POSIX. This is a standard for Unix-like operating systems. If you can find a POSIX-compliant way of doing something then you should be able to make it work on most varieties of Unix and Linux. Even Windows has some POSIX-compliant features.

If a POSIX standard doesn't exist for something then your only real choice is Linux. Linux is by far the most common operating system on servers and on small machines that run an operating system. Making use of a non-POSIX feature doesn't really make your code much less portable.

In this book the emphasis is on standard C. If you want to know more about using C on POSIX-compliant and Linux-based systems, see its companion volume: ***Applying C For The IoT With Linux*** ISBN: 978-1871962611.

Platform Dependent or Independent – Undefined Behavior

One of the big problems with modern C is that there are two distinct types of programmer wanting very different things from it. Applications programmers, and to an extent systems programmers, would like C to be platform independent. This basically means that they are free to write their programs without considering the architecture of the machine it is running on. To a lesser extent they can also ignore differences in operating systems, but only really to different flavors of Linux. If the target machine is running Windows then no matter how machine independent the language is, your code has to take the differences into account.

It is clear that there are different levels of platform independence, but a significant number of users are convinced that nothing in the C language should be machine dependent. As a result, the C standards identify behavior that is likely to be machine dependent and mark it as undefined behavior. As the behavior is undefined it should never occur in a correct program.

The big problem is that undefined behavior has been taken to mean "any behavior at all". This has given compiler writers a free hand to make anything at all happen as the result of a program that has undefined behavior and, as will be explained later, this means optimization can have very unexpected consequences. It is true to say that undefined behavior is one of the biggest problems C programmers have at the moment – at least in theory. In practice things are rarely so extreme, but you need to know about this as early as possible.

By contrast there is a second group of programmers who don't want the language to be machine independent. They want C to allow the natural machine behavior in each situation. The fact that this means that the language is defined in a different way depending on the platform the program is running on is seen as the price you have to pay to gain access to the machine's behavior. To illustrate, if I'm coding on a specific machine and signed overflow occurs then the result depends on the hardware used to perform arithmetic, and what representation of negative numbers it uses. Just letting the machine do what is natural is perfectly acceptable and even desirable. It is certainly infinitely preferable than the actual solution, which is to make signed integer overflow officially undefined behavior. This means that the compiler writer can legally change the code to make anything happen. As a result undefined behavior is also known as "nasal demons" after a public suggestion that even demons flying out of your nose is acceptable as an interpretation of such a program. A more reasonable interpretation is that any program that contains undefined behavior is an incorrect program. This would be fine if compilers flagged undefined behavior as errors rather than optimizing it in ways that leave the programmer mystified.

Less controversially but equally troubling is the way the compiler writers can assume that in a correctly written program undefined behavior will never occur. For example, by having signed overflow as undefined behavior, the compiler is free to move the value in question to a machine register that is perhaps bigger than the variable that has been assigned to hold the value. The result is that the program runs faster, and the program has to be valid because signed overflow is undefined behavior and therefore cannot happen in a correct program.

Of course, low-level programmers often make use of signed overflow as part of a correct algorithm and when it doesn't happen as expected, because the value is in a register that is big enough not to overflow, then things don't go according to plan. It seems that the requirement of the low-level programmer to have the machine do exactly what the program tells it are overruled by the need of the compiler writers to optimize the output code.

This battle has been going on for longer than undefined behavior.

For example, low-level programmers often use empty loops to "busy wait", i.e. to use up some time. This is fine, but when an optimizing compiler scrutinizes the code it decides that the empty loop isn't doing anything and removes it. The result isn't an optimized program; it is a broken program.

If all of this seems silly, then most programmers would agree. The problem is that the two groups don't see the problem in the same way and each regards the other as trying to ruin a perfectly good language.

For the low-level programmer working close to the machine's hardware, the idea that C should be machine-independent is not an obvious thought. It might not even be possible. For example, the C standard could mandate that signed arithmetic overflow was done in a particular way. This would make C machine-independent but it would put a big overhead on any machine that did signed arithmetic in a different way.

There are times when it seems that the low-level programmer is doing battle with the compiler writers and the language designers and there is a very real sense in which this is true. There are many idioms used by low-level programmers that have been in use for a long time and yet are undefined behavior according to the latest standards. When there are alternative ways of implementing the same behavior then it is a good idea to make use of them. When there isn't, you have no choice but to carry on using them no matter what the standards say. As C continues to evolve, this problem is likely to get worse not better.

Safe Coding

There is a general feeling that C is not a safe language. As already mentioned, the fact that C lets you do almost anything is an invitation to get things very wrong. The most commonly quoted example is the buffer overrun. In many modern languages you can rely on the compiler to make sure that you do not try to access data beyond the limits of the memory assigned to your program. This is not the case with C. A buffer overrun is where the program reads or writes beyond the end of the allocated buffer and it is one of the most common ways that "hackers" attack programs. Of course, in a well-written program, buffer overruns shouldn't happen, but most programs are not well-written.

C is not a language that has built-in safety because automatic safety is mostly bought at the cost of complexity and restrictions, and this is not what C is all about. In addition, if you are using C to access low-level features and hardware then not only do you make the system vulnerable to attack; you can actually physically destroy it, in some cases.

Safety doesn't come with hardware programming unless you work at it.

There are programmers who advocate a more sophisticated and safer language such as Rust, which is one alternative. However, if you need C and you want to write secure code, you need to learn how to do it and preferably use tools to check that you are writing good code. There are a number of well-known guides to writing secure code and you can see an up-to-date list in the Resource section at www.i-programmer.info.

Summary

- C is a language that is closer to the machine hardware than most other languages.

- C is worth learning if you want to understand how computers work at the lowest level.

- C is worth learning if you want to write programs that interact with the hardware.

- Working with the hardware gives rise to a particular form of low-level programming where bit patterns and how the data is represented are important.

- In addition to the original version of C usually called K&R C, there are three important standards - C89, C99 and C11. There is also C18 which is a bug fix to C11.

- C11/C18 is the latest, but some of its features are flawed and many programmers prefer to use C99 as their standard.

- You will encounter C programs written in all forms of C, so you can't really insulate yourself from the past.

- There are two types of C programmer with different requirements. The applications (high-level) programmer wants C to be machine independent and the low-level programmer wants C to convey the essence of the machine in any particular case.

- Currently the machine independent view holds sway and this has resulted in many idioms becoming outlawed as "undefined behavior".

- Undefined behavior is biggest problem in using C in a modern context. A program that contains undefined behavior can be optimized in ways that change its meaning.

- Long before undefined behavior became a problem, compiler writers were sufficiently out of touch with the needs and practices of the low-level coder to optimize away meaningful constructs such as null loops used for timing.

- C is a powerful language and this makes it easy to introduce serious security flaws. You need to be aware of how your program could be misused.

Chapter 2

Getting Started

We all have to start somewhere and in this case I recommend using the standard GCC compiler and the NetBeans IDE. If you already have a C toolchain set up and you are familiar with the process of editing and compiling a program, skip to the next chapter, but if you don't use an IDE, and NetBeans in particular, it might still be worth finding out what you are missing.

NetBeans and GCC

You can program C using nothing more than a text editor and the command line, but this is not as productive as using an IDE (Integrated Development Environment). This is an arguable point if you are a C expert, but for the beginner and the casual user there is no doubt that an IDE is the best way to go. An IDE will not only allow you to edit your program, it will automate the compile and run process and provide you with lots of help on the way.

There is a commonly expressed opinion that you don't need an IDE to program in C. This is quite true. You *can* program in C using nothing but a text editor and the compilers and other tools used from the command line and you should know how to do this. However, programming is hard enough without working with one hand tied behind your back. You should accept any tools you can find that make it easier to create, and almost more importantly maintain, a program.   A modern IDE will provide code highlighting and autocomplete that makes it much harder to make a silly error. It will also point out common problems and bad practices to help you keep your code clean.

Perhaps the biggest reason for using an IDE, however, is to gain easy access to a debugger. As with the use of IDEs, some say you don't need a debugger and can get by with printing variable values to a console. It is claimed that a debugger presents you with far too much information and leads to unfocused exploration of your program. This is nonsense. A good debugger will allow you set breakpoints, i.e. points in your program where it will pause and allow you examine what is stored in variables. This is only unfocused if you are, and it only provides too much information if you have no clue what you are looking for. Add to this the facility to step instruction by instruction though a program and you have a tool that can save you hours and ensure that your program is working. While you can use a debugger without an IDE, the whole experience is so much easier that you are more likely to use the facilities. In short, only an idiot would turn down the help of a good IDE.

But which IDE?

This is also a question about which compiler to use. Not all IDEs support every compiler and so you are choosing an IDE/compiler pair.

If you are working with Windows then there is tendency to choose Visual Studio Community edition. It is free to use, but it supports so many options that it can be confusing. There is also the small matter that Microsoft is really more interested in C++ than C. Currently its C compiler only supports as much C89 as needed to make C++ work - but this is getting better. You can also install an add-in that lets you develop C programs that run under Linux, but the Microsoft C compiler is strictly an 86x compiler.

The main workhorse of the C world is the GCC (GNU Compiler Collection), which can be used to target a range of different CPUs. Ideally you need an IDE that is primarily designed to work with GCC or a derivative of it.

GCC is standard on Linux and many other operating systems, but it isn't standard on Windows. Another problem is that it doesn't come with an IDE. Fine if you want to use the command line and a text editor, but as already discussed, not so good if you want to write C only occasionally.

There are a number of different IDEs that can make use of the GCC – Geany, Eclipse, C Lion and even Microsoft's Visual Studio Code. A good all-rounder, and one that can be used with multiple languages on multiple platforms, is Apache NetBeans - it also happens to be free to use and open source. You can use NetBeans to program in Java, JavaScript with HTML/CSS, C/C++, Fortran, Assembler and PHP. It also installs a standard C debugger without any fuss and this makes it well worth getting to know.

In the rest of this book NetBeans is the IDE in use, but as it really only makes an impact in this chapter you can feel free to use whatever IDE you care to adopt.

NetBeans C/C++ Under Linux and Windows

Using NetBeans under Linux or Windows is so trivial that it almost doesn't need any additional explanation. All you have to do is download a version of NetBeans from:

`https://netbeans.apache.org/`

The latest version 10 only downloads in a base version and you have to add the necessary plugin for C/C++. At the time of writing you have to use the plugin for version 8 but this may change in future. There is no installer for NetBeans from version 9 on. Simply download the ZIP file and expand it into a suitable folder. Under Windows you can use:

`\Program Files\NetBeans10`

or whatever the version number is.

To get a shortcut to run the program, drag a link from the bin subdirectory using `netbeans.exe` or `netbeans64.exe`. You can have multiple NetBeans versions installed at the same time.

Once you have NetBeans installed use the Tools/Plugins menu item and select the Settings tab. Select the NetBeans 8.2 Plugin Portal or if not available for some reason use the URL:

`http://updates.netbeans.org/netbeans/updates/8.2/`
                    `uc/final/distribution/catalog.xml.gz`

Look in the list of available plugins and install the C/C++ plugin. When this is completed you will be able to create and work with a C/C++ project.

Installing GCC

As already mentioned, the most common choice of C compiler is the GNU Compiler Collection (GCC) and this needs to be installed.

Under Linux there should be nothing to do as GCC is usually installed by default - it is certainly standard on Ubuntu, Raspbian and more. If not you have to use whatever packet manager your distribution uses to install it.

Under Windows we have a very different story. GCC is a Linux compiler and you need some Linux utilities such as `make.o` to get it working. There are many different ways to get GCC running under Windows and everyone has their own favorite. Mine is MinGW- it really is minimal and doesn't make a mess of your Windows installation. However, it is important that you get the right version.

Go to http://www.mingw.org/ and download a file called `mingw-get-setup.exe` or similar. This is the graphical installer and when it is downloaded you should run it.

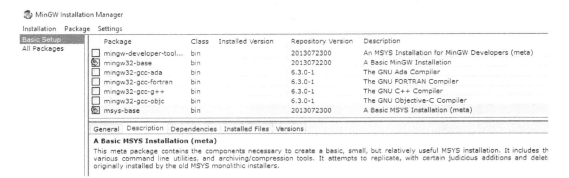

Select Basic Setup to install `mingw32-base` which contains the GCC compilers and `msys-base` which contains make. When the installer completes the installation you can move on to trying out NetBeans.

Windows 10 also has the Linux subsystem and you might be tempted to explore this route to getting GCC, but there are complications. If you enable the Linux subsystem you should find that GCC is installed by default. If not you can install it using a package manager such as `apt-get`. You can use GCC from the command line without doing anything extra, but it is a Linux compiler and creates only Linux programs.

That is, you can run your compiled code under the Linux subsystem, but not under Windows. You can even install NetBeans and use it to create programs, but these will only run under Linux. If this is what you want then no problem, but using a Linux machine, as a Virtual Machine if necessary, is a much more direct way to use Linux software.

The MinGW installation provides you with a Windows version of GCC that allows you to create programs that run under Windows using a Windows version of NetBeans. That is, it creates Windows executables.

A First Program

Now that you we have a machine with GCC installed plus the necessary tools that NetBeans uses, we can try to create a first program to make sure everything is working.

Load NetBeans and select `File, New Project`. Select `C/C++ Application` in the dialog box that appears:

Move on to the next step by clicking `Next`. The dialog box that appears allows you to name the project - `HelloWorld` is a good choice:

Notice that we have selected C99 as the language we are going to use.
The important entry in this dialog is `Tool Collection`, which should show that a tool collection is in use - in this case MinGW under Windows. If there are multiple tool collections select the appropriate one for the machine you are targeting. Finally if you now click `Finish` a project will be created.

Using Tool Collections

If you encounter a problem with tool collections at this point it is probably better to cancel the project creation and move to the Services window to examine the Tool Collections available.

You can see the tool collections that are locally installed and any that are installed on remote servers. Using a remote build server is a perfectly good way to learn C programming, but a local tool collection is perhaps easier.

If you are developing programs for IoT devices then you will almost certainly need to use either a cross-compiler or a remote build server. For example, if you are using a Raspberry Pi then the easiest thing to do is to use the GCC tool collection installed by default on the Pi. NetBeans will automatically download your source code, compile it on the Pi and then run it.

For simplicity let's use a local tool collection. If you right click on a tool collection and select Properties then the dialog box that appears tells you where each of the components of GCC and the Make utility are located.

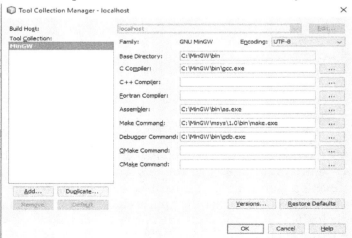

24

If you know better then change the entries. More commonly, if NetBeans has failed to automatically find any of the components, it is up to you to supply their locations.

In the case of MinGW, if anything is missing, the simplest option is to go back to the installer and try again. As long as you are using the correct version of MinGW, NetBeans should just work.

Remote C/C++ Build Servers

Creating and using a remote build server is slightly more complicated than working with a local machine and if you are just getting to grips with NetBeans then come back to this section later.

NetBeans is an excellent way to create programs for SBCs that are big enough to host their own GCC or other compiler toolchain, but are not really powerful enough to run an IDE like NetBeans. In this case the best way to work is to use NetBeans on a desktop machine and use the SBC as a remote build server.

NetBeans supports two remote build host modes:

- SSH file copying
- Directory sharing

Of the two, SSH file copying is the easier to get started with, but it can be slow and files that you change in the IDE have to be copied to the remote build host every time you compile the project. To make directory sharing work, you have to know how to connect to a remote directory on both the local and the remote system.

In most cases, SSH file copying is the best choice as it makes switching target machines very easy. You can set up multiple build servers and change the target of a project to test on different machine just by changing the build server. The files on the local machine are copied as needed to the target machine.

To set up a remote build server that uses SSH file copying you need to have the remote Linux machine, a Raspberry Pi in our example, set up correctly, connected to the local network and accessible using SSH.

Your first task is to create a build host. To do this use the menu command:

`Window,Services`

and drop down `C/C++ Build Hosts` in the window that appears.

If you are running NetBeans on a desktop machine you might see some compilers or, under Windows, you will see None(No Compilers Found).

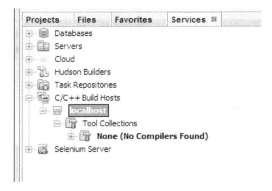

To work remotely we need to add the Pi as a build server. To do this right click on C/C++ Build Hosts and select Add New Host:

The dialog box that appears lets you set the identity of the build server.

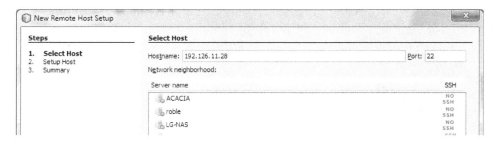

In most cases you will have to supply the IP address of the Pi unless you have set up Samba on it. There are advantages to doing this, but not when you are just getting started. The next dialog box that appears lets you type in a user name and specify how authentication will proceed. You can use a key file but in the first instance just use a password.

You can use the default log-in details of user name "pi" and password "raspberry". Notice that these are both case sensitive. You will be asked for the password when you first connect to the Pi – and it is, of course, the password that the user you specified needs to log into the Pi. This may seem obvious, but with so many users and passwords involved in setting things up it can be confusing.

The final dialog box presents you with a summary of what you have set up:

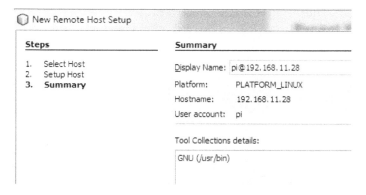

NetBeans should have found the C compiler and linker you are going to use as part of the GNU Collection. In a more general situation you might have to tell NetBeans where the compiler is, or select which set of tools you want to use. In the case of the Pi and Raspbian you can leave the defaults as they are.

If you now create a new project you can test out the new build host.

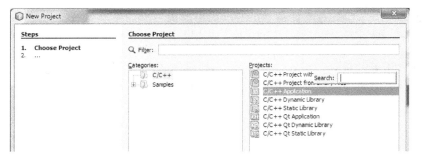

Select File.New Project followed by C/C++ Application. The next dialog box is where you customize the project. You can give the project any name you like and "HelloC" is reasonable for this first example. You need to select the dialect of C you are working in and C99 is a common choice. You can generally leave the rest of the entries at their defaults. Finally you to set the Build Host from the default Localhost to the build host you set up earlier.

Now you can makes some changes to the project and run the program. When you do this any files that you have edited are copied to a corresponding folder in your home Linux directory. In this case HelloC.c is copied from the directory NetBeansProjects\HelloC to /home/pi/NetBeansProjects/HelloC. If the folders on the Linux machine don't exist then they are created.

NetBeans uses SFTP to copy the files and then it uses SSH to send commands to the build host to compile the files stored on the remote and run them on the remote. As SFTP depends on SSH, you can see that if SSH isn't working then you won't even get as far as copying the files.

About the only thing that can go wrong if SSH is working is that NetBeans will fail to copy the files. This is usually a permissions problem and you need to make sure that the user you have specified in the build host setup can create folders and files in their home directory which, of course, should always be possible.

NetBeans doesn't always get which files to copy correct and this is one of the reasons why the file sharing method of remote building is often preferred. If this happens then simply perform a clean build.

There is also the small problem of working with custom libraries. In this case the library file has to be installed on the remote machine. The header file for the library also has to be available on the local machine if NetBeans is to understand the code before it is compiled.

Creating a Hello World Program

If all of this works it is now time for the easy part - creating the Hello World program.

Go back to the Projects tab, drop down the Source Files node in the Projects window and select main.c. This will open in the editor. Change the program to read:

```
13
14  ⊟  #include <stdio.h>
15  └  #include <stdlib.h>
16
17  ⊟  /*
18  │    *
19  └    */
20  ⊟  int main(int argc, char** argv) {
21  │       printf("hello C World");
22  │       return (EXIT_SUCCESS);
23  └  }
24
```

In other words, add:

```
printf("hello C World");
```

to the program. Now click the green arrow compile and run button or use Run, Run Project or press F6 and your program will be compiled and run. You will see the output in the Output window at the bottom of the screen. You will also see a lot of other messages scroll past before your program is run - what some of these mean will be explained in later chapters.

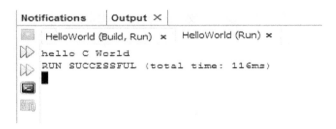

If you have a working C compiler you are now ready and equipped to move on to the next stage and start learning some C.

From the Command Line

You can compile using nothing but the command line. First use a text editor of your choice to create the `main.c` file and save it.

From the command prompt use:

```
gcc main.c -o main
```

This compiles `main.c` to an executable called `main`. The `-o` is a command line option that sets the name of the output file. There are many additional options you can specify.

To run the program under Linux simply type:

```
./main
```

and you should see the hello world message. If this doesn't work the chances are that the path isn't set correctly and the system cannot find GCC.

At this point you might be thinking that the command line option is simpler than setting up an IDE, but as your programs become more complex the command line approach becomes increasingly complicated and error prone.

For more information on how the compiler works, see Chapter 14.

Summary

- Setting up an IDE is an effort well worth the expense. It will save you a lot of time in the future.

- There are many C compilers, but GCC is available on a very wide range of machines and it is the one to use unless you have a good reason not to.

- To make GCC work under Windows, a simple solution is to use MinGW.

- There are many alternative IDEs, but NetBeans is open source and it works well with GCC on Windows and Linux.

- NetBeans will automatically find the GCC toolset on the local machine.

- You can also make use of a remote machine as a build server. NetBeans will upload the program to the remote machine and use GCC to compile it and run it.

- For a simple program such as "hello world" the GCC compiler can be used from the command line.

Chapter 3

Control Structures and Data

This chapter is an introduction to the very basics of programming in C. It covers the least you have to know to begin creating a program - variables, conditionals and loops. If you are already a C programmer then you will already know most of this and you can skip to the next chapter. However, while this chapter is at an introductory level, it includes explanations of how things work that you might not be familiar with. and that will help in the remainder of this book.

Variables, assignment and expressions

Before we can move on and look at instructions - the verbs of the program - we have to have something for them to work with - the nouns of the program. Data is covered in more detail in the next chapter, but we cannot even start on C without some basic ideas of variables and data. This is a very basic and incomplete first look at the topic.

The fundamental entity in C is the variable, which, roughly speaking, is a chunk of storage that you have given a name to. What you can store there depends on what you specify when you create the variable. For example, in C, and most modern languages, you can store an integer (whole number) value in an `int` variable (`int` is just short for integer).

So, for example:

```
int a;
```

creates a variable called a that you can store an integer in.

Notice that the line ends with a semicolon. In C you can split instructions across multiple lines as it is only the semicolon which is used to mark the end of a logical line. In the same way you can group instructions on a single line separating them by semicolons.

How do you store a value in a variable? You use the assignment operator "=".

For example:

```
a=10;
```

isn't a statement that a is equal to ten, it is an instruction to store the value 10 in the variable a.

Understanding what is going on becomes much easier if you always read the equals as "assign to" as in "assign 10 to a" or "store in" as in "store 10 in a". (The point is never read it as "a equals 10" because this could be a statement or a question.)

A variable can only store one value at a time so if you store another value in it then anything already stored is lost.

For example:

```
a=20;
```

stores 20 in a and any record of the 10 previously stored is lost.

Most programmers who have been working with variables quickly forget that there is any other way it could be done and might even wonder why I'm bothering to tell you all this.

If you are happy with these basic ideas then we can add two more observations. You can both create and store a value in a variable at the same time.

That is instead of writing:

```
int a;
a=1;
```

you can write:

```
int a=1;
```

as a shorthand.

The second idea is slightly more complicated. You can use a variable on both sides of an assignment.

For example:

```
a=b;
```

retrieves the value stored in b and stores it in a. After this instruction a and b store the same value. (Again it is important not to read this as "a equals b" but "store the contents of b in a". Remember, it is a command not a description.)

You can also write things like:

```
a=2*4+b;
```

Here the right-hand side contains an arithmetic expression that will be worked out and stored in a. Notice you can use variables on the right-hand side and their values will be retrieved and used in the calculation.

You can generally write arithmetic expressions as you would normally, but notice that the multiplication sign is * (an asterisk) and the division sign is /. Also feel free to use parentheses to make sure things are worked out in the correct order. C has a very large number of operators that go well beyond the well-known operations of arithmetic. We have much more to say about operators and expressions in Chapters 4, 5 and 6.

An expression can be thought of as a mini-program. It is a recipe for how to combine values stored in variables and constants to produce a new value.

An arithmetic expression that causes a lot of problems when you first see it is:

```
a=a+1;
```

Which if you read it as "a equals a plus one" sounds like nonsense. What it does is to increase the value stored in a by one, i.e. it increments the value in a. If you read it as "retrieve the value in a, add one to it and store the result back in a", then all should be clear.

Adding one to a variable is so common that C has a special operator for it:

```
a++;
```

or

```
++a;
```

is the same as:

```
a=a+1;
```

The difference between the two forms will be explained in Chapter 6.

There are lots of different types of data that can be stored in a variable, but for the moment integer variables will serve well as an example.

Now we have something to write instructions about, let's see what sort of things we can do.

Program Structure

The first thing we need to look at it what makes a minimum program in C.

If you start a new project in NetBeans, the system automatically generates a file containing:

```
#include <stdio.h>
#include <stdlib.h>
int main(int argc, char** argv) {
    return (EXIT_SUCCESS);
}
```

This is the most basic of C programs. It is simple, but it contains features that will only become clear after we have looked at quite a lot more C.

The `#include` instructions automatically include the files specified, i.e. `stdio.h` and `stdlib.h`. These files are read into your program file as if you had written what they contain into your file. This is the standard way of getting library files into your program. There is more to say about this, but for the moment all that matters is that you understand that including a file is a way to access existing code contained in the standard C libraries or third party libraries. See Chapter 14 for an in-depth explanation of includes.

Using libraries is important in C because the language itself is very simple and has few facilities. It is a minimalist language so many of the features that you need to make C a useful language are provided by its libraries. For example, C has no statements or commands that relate to I/O - no print or input commands. These are simply not part of the C language and in this sense they are not "standard". However, the I/O functions that you find in the standard library might as well be part of the language because they are what every C programmer uses.

C makes use of a function called `main` to determine where to start executing your program. You can specify the name of the function where you want your program to start using an argument passed to the compiler, but most C programs start at `main`.

The only complication with `main` are its parameters. The first, `int argc` is easy, it is the number of parameters passed to `main` from the command line. The second is slightly more difficult to explain this early, but it is essentially an array containing the command line parameters specified by the user. We can return to this when we have explained how arrays work in Chapter 8.

The main program always returns an integer to indicate success or failure. A zero is success and any other value is considered to be an error code. This is what return `EXIT_SUCCESS` does for you - it returns a zero to indicate that everything has worked. Notice that we use the constant `EXIT_SUCCESS`. Again this is not part of the language but it is defined in `stdlib` - more about this sort of constant in Chapter 14.

You could just as well write:

```
return 0;
```

Comments

It is worth mentioning that you can add comments to a program that are ignored by the compiler. Anything between /* and /* will be ignored by the compiler and this includes multiple lines.

For example:

```
/*  this is a comment */
```

and

```
/* this
    is a
    comment
    too */
```

C99 introduced single line comments using //. Everything following the double slash is a comment to the end of the line. For example:

```
// this is a comment
```

and

```
int x,y; // x,y are the coordinates of a point
```

As the double slash is the standard way of commenting in C++ many programmers think it should be in C, but it is only in C99 and later.

At this point most books explain how important comments are and how you should use them as much as possible, resulting in commented code such as:

```
a=a+1; //add one to a
```

Personally I disagree and instead advocate code that can be easily read and understood. To achieve this, first make your code as intelligible as possible by using good variable names and a clear layout. Never take a short cut or use a trick if it makes your code harder to understand. Clear code is almost self-commenting. Only add comments where the intent of your code isn't clear or to point out any potential problems that might arise in the future.

It is important to write comments that make the intent of you code clear. Say what you are trying to do and give the overall design of the program. Instead of spending hours adding comments that don't add much, take the time to write proper documentation for your code.

The Flow of Control

If you look at any list of instructions, i.e. any program in the widest possible sense, you'll see that there are only a few ways that the instructions can be organized. Even if you are a skilled programmer this may not have been pointed out to you explicitly. If you are not a skilled programmer then be aware that this is the very skill of programming. There are just three basic approaches to presenting a list of instructions, even in a natural language:

- ◆ You can write a one-after-the-other list.
- ◆ You can write a conditional list, for example:
  "if it is raining then pick up the umbrella"
- ◆ You can specify a repetition, for example:
  "keep stirring your coffee until the sugar dissolves"

37

These three are the only possible forms that a list of instructions can take and it can be proved that if you have these three forms then you can write any program that can exist.

A language that has these three things is said to be "Turing complete", after the mathematician and early computer pioneer Alan Turing. You might be able to guess that C is indeed Turing complete and has all three forms.

This observation is also the basis of the structured programming philosophy that aims to restrict programming and programmers to just these three fundamental forms clearly expressed. While you can invent other more complicated instructions, these are the "programming atoms" from which all other programs can be constructed.

If you have a list of instructions in front of you then you can follow the order of execution of the instructions, or the "flow of control", simply by tracing your finger along the instructions in the order that they are carried out. The resulting shape is called the "flow of control graph" and it is fundamental to programming.

If you understand how to build a flow of control graph that does a particular job, you are a programmer, and if you don't, you aren't.

The three fundamental flow of control forms correspond to a straight line segment following the one after the other order of instructions, a branching structure that divides between alternative lists of instructions and a circular looping shape that indicates the repetition of instructions.

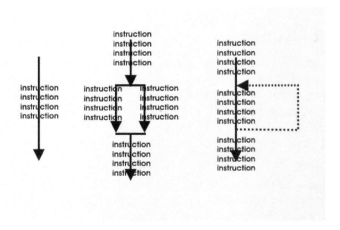

All programming languages have instructions which are obeyed one after another. In C a sequence of statements have to be separated by a semicolon. For example:

```
instruction1;
instruction2;
instruction3;
```

is a program that does instruction1, followed by 2 and finally 3. As already mentioned the semicolons are statement separators and they are the only thing C takes notice of - white space and new lines are just ignored.

So you could write:

```
instruction1;instruction2;instruction3;
```

In most cases it is better to write one instruction per line and only group things together on a single line if it helps understanding.

For example:

```
a=b+c;
d=e+f;
```

is better over two lines as the two statements have nothing to do with each other, but:

```
x=23;y=100;
```

make sense on the same line if x and y are the coordinates of a point and hence logically used together.

This is something programmers can, and do, argue about.

The most important thing is to try to write C that is maximally understandable and any formatting that you can use to make things clear is a good thing. Cramming everything into one line just to save space on the page is always a bad thing.

Executing one instruction after another is known as the "default flow of control". As the program is executed only one instruction has the attention of the processor at any moment and this is the instruction that is said to be in "control". Control passes through the program from left to right and top to bottom in the usual order that English is read.

As well as the default flow of control all computer languages have two other patterns of flow of control - the conditional and the loop.

Let's see how C deals with each of these.

The Conditional

In most computer languages the conditional is implemented using some construct involving the words "if" and "else".

In C the simplest if statement is:

```
if(condition) instruction;
```

The instruction is only carried out if the condition is true.

For example:

```
if(x>10) y=5;
```

Although we haven't covered very much C, this should be understandable. The variable y is only set to five if x is greater than 10. The instruction is skipped if the condition isn't true.

This simple form of if statement is enough for many situations, it is the one you will use the most, but sometimes you want to do one instruction if the condition is true and a different one if it is false. In this case you need the else statement:

```
if(condition) instruction1;else instruction2;
```

Now instruction1 is carried out if the condition is true and instruction2 if it is false. Notice that only one of instruction1 or instruction2 will be carried out.

You write conditions in much the way that you would in arithmetic. For example x>10 is true if x is greater than 10.

The comparison operators are:

```
>     greater than
<     less than
>=    greater than or equal
<=    less than or equal
==    equal to
!=    not equal to
```

Notice that == (two equals signs) is a test of equality and = is an assignment.

It is really important to make sure that you understand and remember the difference.

Even if you do understand the difference, you will occasionally get things wrong if only by mistyping.

Notice that:

```
a==0;
```

is true if a contains 0 and:

```
a=0;
```

stores 0 in a.

Look out for the common error:

```
if(a=0)...
```

Once you know how to write a condition you can start using if statements. For example:

```
if(x>10) y=5; else y=0;
```

sets y to 5 if x is greater than 10 and sets y to 0 if it isn't.

You can write the if..else construct on separate lines and this looks better and is easier to read:

```
if(x>10) y=5;
else y=0;
```

Notice that:

```
if(x>10) y=5; else y=0;
```

is not the same as:

```
if(x>10) y=5;
y=0;
```

The first one sets y to 5 or 0 depending on the value of x. The second always sets y to 0 after sometimes setting it to 5.

The Compound Statement

You may be wondering how C copes with the problem of conditionally executing any number of statements.

The if and the else only let you write a single statement after them. This seems to be very limited, but C has a powerful idea that simplifies many things. You can use curly brackets to group any number of instructions together to make a compound statement.

A compound statement is treated as if it was a single statement.

That is:

```
{instruction1;instruction2;instruction3;}
```

is composed of three separate instructions but it is treated as a single statement.

You don't need a semicolon at the end of a compound statement as the closing bracket signifies the end of the statement. Also notice that the last instruction in the list has to have a semicolon terminator.

So you can now write:

```
if (condition){instruction1;instruction2;instruction3;}
```

and instructions 1 through 3 will be carried out if and only if the condition is true.

You can format this as:

```
if (condition){
  instruction1;
  instruction2;
  instruction3;
}
```

This is the way that NetBeans will format the if for you and it is the most common way to write it. Notice that the indenting makes it easier to see the start and end of the if statement.

To get NetBeans to format your program simply use the command Source, Format or right click and select Format. The shortcut is Alt-Shift-F. Autoformatting is a surprisingly good way of finding errors in your code. If NetBeans doesn't format it the way you expect then you have entered something incorrectly.

Using compound statements in the if..else construct you can write things like:

```
if (condition){
  instruction1;
  instruction2;
  instruction3;
} else {
  instruction4;
  instruction5;
}
```

This will carry out instructions 1,2 and 3 if the condition is true and 4 and 5 if it is false.

This too is the way NetBeans will format the code for you, although there are arguments that other ways are better. The best practice is to select a formatting rule and stick to it and avoid getting into arguments about which format is best.

The simple if and the if..else cover most of the situations you encounter. More advanced conditionals are covered later in this chapter.

Loops

All languages have some way of repeating a block of code and it is fundamental to programming.

There are two distinct types of loop – the enumeration loop and the conditional loop.

An enumeration loop is where you repeat something a given known number of times, for example, "stir your coffee three times".

A conditional loop is where you repeat something an undetermined number of times until some condition is satisfied, for example, "stir your coffee until the sugar has dissolved".

You can probably see at once that the conditional loop is really the only one you need as an enumeration loop is just a conditional loop that stops when the number of repeats has been achieved. Even so most programming languages provide a construct for enumeration loops and one or more for conditional loops.

While it is theoretically possible to do everything you need to do with just one type of loop, most languages provide more for ease of use and C has three types - the for loop, the while loop and the do while loop.

Of the three, the C for loop is the most complicated and is confusing to programmers from many other languages. Its strange form is due to the way it relates to the underlying machine language and once you know this then it is perfectly simple and logical. So with this in mind let's start our look at loops with the most complicated.

The for loop

If you want to do an instruction three times you could achieve that simply by writing it three times:

```
instruction;
instruction;
instruction;
```

However, this isn't a clever way to work and it quickly becomes increasingly difficult as the number of repeats goes up. There is an old programming joke:

> "I wrote a program that was one million lines long – and then I discovered the for loop."

To allow you to repeat an action a set number of times most modern languages provide a for loop - the reason for the name will become apparent very soon.

The problem is that the C style for loop is very flexible but it can seem complex to the beginner. We'll start by looking at an example before seeing the general form.

Consider:

```
for(int counter=0; counter<10; counter++)instruction;
```

This will repeat the single instruction ten times. However, it is more common to use a compound instruction to repeat a block of code:

```
for(int counter=0; counter<10;counter++){
   instructions to repeat;
}
```

Note: you can only declare the variable counter within the loop in C99 and later. In earlier versions of C the variable has to be declared before the loop. When declared in the loop the variable overrides any variable of the same name and is destroyed when the loop ends, see Block Scope in Chapter 7.

When the for loop is obeyed the counter variable is first set to 0 as specified by the first part of the loop:

```
for(int counter=0; counter<10;counter++)
```

Then the test specified:

```
for(int counter=0;counter<10;counter++)
```

is evaluated. If it is true the "body" of the loop is obeyed. If it is false then the loop comes to an end and if this is the first time the for loop has been encountered the body of the loop is skipped.

If the condition is true then the instructions in the loop are carried out. When these are completed the counter has one added to it as specified by the final part of the for:

```
for(int counter=0; counter<10;counter++)
```

The ++ operator is the increment operator, introduced earlier, and simply adds one to the value stored in counter. Then the condition counter<10 is evaluated again and if it is true the loop repeats, i.e. the instructions in the body are carried out all over again but this time with counter storing the value 1. If it is false then the loop is complete.

If you think about this mechanism you should be able to see that this will cause the instructions to be repeated for values of "counter" starting at 0 and ending at 9.

Why is 9 the last value?

Simply because when you add 1 to 9 you get 10 and 10 is not smaller than 10 and so counter<10 is false and the loop ends.

So you can just think of the for loop as being a way to repeat a block of code n times:

```
for(int counter=0; counter<n; counter++){
 instructions
}
```

Notice that the loop starts from 0 and it repeats n times. The counter, or more generally the loop index, counts from 0 up to n-1 and hence the loop repeats n times.

Why count from zero?

This is a very old question and it has to do with the way arrays work. It is particularly relevant in C, as will be explained in Chapter 8, but put simply the first element of an array is element zero and so it makes sense to start for loops from zero as arrays and for loops were made for each other.

So when you want to do something n times do it for values of the index from 0 to n-1.

If you really want to you can create a modified loop that starts from 1 and counts to n, but the zero start form is far more common as we shall see.

The general for loop

A more general form of the for loop is:

```
for(int counter=start; counter<end+1; counter++)
```

and can be thought of as being equivalent to "repeat for values of counter from start to end".

If you don't like the "end+1" in the condition you can write the for loop as:

```
for(int counter=start;counter<=end;counter++)
```

where counter<=end is true if counter is smaller than or equal to end. It's all a matter of taste.

However, this isn't the most general form of the for loop even if it is the sort of loop that is used most often.

The most general for loop is:

```
for(initial; condition; increment)
```

In this case the initial instruction is performed once when the loop starts. The condition is evaluated at the start of each repeat of the loop and the loop only continues if it is true. The increment instruction is performed after the loop has executed all of the instructions in the body of the loop and before the next repeat is contemplated.

That is, the algorithm for the for loop is:

1. evaluate the *initial* expressions
2. test the *condition* and if it is false exit the loop i.e. go to step 5
3. perform the actions in the body of the loop
4. execute the *increment* expression and return to step 2
5. rest of program

Notice that this means that if the condition is initially true then the body of the loop will never be carried out. That is, the smallest number of times a for loop can execute is zero and a for loop can repeat something zero or more times.

For example if you run:

```
for(int i=0;i>1;i++){
    printf("loop");
}
```

you will not see "loop" printed because the condition is already false.

Also notice that there is no need for the increment expression to actually increment anything or for the condition to test anything that relates to it. You can write any expression you like – they don't have to make sense or do anything particularly useful. Of course in practice they usually do something useful even if what it is isn't immediately obvious.

This form of the for loop is capable of being used in many wonderful ways and some C programmers delight in finding new ways of using it.

For example, what do you think:

```
for(;;){body of loop}
```

does?

It is an infinite loop, i.e. one that never ends. It has no initialization statement, no test and so by default always true, and no increment. Although slightly cryptic, this is a fairly common idiom in IoT programs which are often designed to repeat the same actions over and over.

Good style suggests that you should stick to simple for loops.

If you find the for loop difficult to grasp or to remember then don't worry. Most uses of the for loop are simple and just about repeating a block of instructions a number of times. The for loop is also made to go with another programming idea - the array, see Chapter 8. In this case the counter, or index variable, is used to specify which of a list of values you are processing.

The goto and the for

As already discussed, the C for loop is a little strange in that it is much more general than a for loop found in many other languages. The reason is that it corresponds reasonably closely to the way that loops are created in assembly or lower level languages using a goto or jump instruction. C has a goto instruction, which is best avoided, but it demonstrates how a for loop translates to something simpler.

The principle of a goto is very simple. You place a label to mark a location within your program and then use goto label to transfer control to that location. A label is a name ending in a colon placed at the start of an instruction.

For example:

```
goto label;
  .   .   .

label: instruction;
```

when the program reaches the goto the next instruction obeyed is the one associated with the label.

The goto often seems to be powerful and exciting to beginners because it lets you do anything. However, it almost invariably results in a program that is a mess. Don't use it unless you know what you are doing - and if you do know what you are doing you won't want to use it.

We can, however, use the goto to show how the C for loop is implemented in machine code. All machines have a low level equivalent of the goto in their machine code – usually called jump or jmp.

The for loop:

```
for(initial;condition; increment){
    body of loop
}
```

can be written using goto as:

```
initial;
loop: if(!condition) goto exit;
    body of loop
    increment;
goto loop;

exit: rest of program;
```

The only new element here is the use of ! to mean "not". That is, !condition is true if condition is false and false if it is true. There is more on logical operators in the next chapter. Although this is still a C program, it is very close to what the C compiler generates in almost any machine code. It is worth seeing what this looks like, but don't worry if you don't know assembler – come back to this when you do.

For example, the simple loop:

```
    i = 0;
loop:
    if (i > 10) goto exit;
    i++;
    goto loop;
exit:
    rest of program
```

generates the following x86 assembler:

```
!     i = 0;
main+14: movl    $0x0,0x1c(%esp)
!loop:
!     if (i > 10) goto exit;
main+22: cmpl    $0xa,0x1c(%esp)
main+27: jg      0x4014ad <main+36>
!     i++;
main+29: addl    $0x1,0x1c(%esp)
!     goto loop;
main+34: jmp     0x40149f <main+22>
main+36: rest of program
!exit:
```

The output is fairly easy to read once you know that ! is a comment line showing the C instruction that the following assembler implements. The first part of the line gives the current address e.g. main+14: is where the first instruction is stored. After the address we have the assembly language instruction followed by the values it operates on. So:

```
!     i = 0;
main+14: movl    $0x0,0x1c(%esp)
```

means that the assembler implements the C instruction i=0 and it is stored starting at main+14. The instruction is movl which means move long, i.e. a move instruction operating on 32-bit words. The $0x0 is the data, i.e. 0 and the 0x1c(%esp) is the location of the variable i. Hence the assembly language moves 0 into the memory location where i is stored. The notation 0x1c means the number is 1C in hexadecimal see Chapter 5.

The output has been edited to make it clear, but you can see the jmp main+22 makes the loop repeat and the cmpl (compare long) and the jg (jump greater) are equivalent to the if statement that ends the loop. You can also see that the addl (add long) adds $0x01, i.e. 1, to the location that i is stored in and so increments i.

You can see that C instructions you write are very close to the assembly language that the compiler produces. In most cases if you understand your C program, you can understand the assembly that it produces – with the help of a table of assembly language instructions.

Now consider the for loop:

```
for (int counter = 0; counter < 10; counter++) {
    printf("%d", counter);
}
```

Leaving out the code that calls printf, this compiles to:

```
!    for(int counter=0; counter<10;counter++){
main+14: movl    $0x0,0x1c(%esp)
main+22: jmp     0x4014ba <main+49>
main+24: mov     0x1c(%esp),%eax
!  printf("%d",counter);
main+44: addl    $0x1,0x1c(%esp)
main+49: cmpl    $0x9,0x1c(%esp)
main+54: jle     0x4014a1 <main+24>
!}
```

This is a little more convoluted that the first example – the compiler produces efficient code not readable code. The first instruction at main+14 sets the counter to zero, next we jump to main+49 where we compare the counter to 9 and jump back to main+24 if it is less than 9. At instruction main+24 we pass the counter to the call to printf, add one to the counter and repeat the compare. You can see that this is very similar to our first example but with a slightly modified logic for efficiency reasons.

The point is that the C for loop corresponds closely to the way that a loop is implemented in assembler and this is why the C for loop is the way that it is.

While loop

The for loop is designed to allow you to repeat a block of code a set number of times, but this isn't the most general type of loop. More general is the conditional loop that repeats a block of code until a condition is satisfied. The for loop is like the instruction to "eat three sweets", whereas the conditional loop is more like "eat sweets while you are hungry".

The basic C conditional loop is the while loop and, as its name suggests, it keeps repeating an instruction while a condition is true.

That is:

```
while(condition) instruction;
```

will repeat the instruction over and over again until the condition is false. That is, the condition is evaluated, if it is true the instruction is obeyed, then the condition is evaluated and if it is true the instruction is obeyed and so on. The repeat stops when the condition evaluates to false.

Repeating a single instruction isn't as common as repeating a block of instructions using a compound instruction. So:

```
while(condition){
   instructions
}
```

will repeat the instructions over and over again until the condition is false.

For example:

```
a=1;
while(a<10){
   a++;
}
```

This is also how NetBeans will automatically format a while loop for you. This assigns one to a, then tests to see if a is less than 10, it is so the loop is carried out and a is incremented, i.e. a has two stored in it. The loop goes back to the start and the condition is evaluated and again a is less than 10 so the loop proceeds.

You should be able to see that the loop is repeated until a reaches 10 so the loop repeats for values of a from 1 to 9.

In this case the while loop is equivalent to a for loop:

```
for(a=1;a<10;a++){
```

However, in general you can write while loops that are not simple "repeat a set number of times". It is in this sense that a while loop is more general than a for loop.

Notice that if the condition if false when the loop starts then the loop body will be skipped. That is, a while loop can execute the loop body zero or more times.

It is also worth noting that the general while loop is equivalent to:

```
for(;condition;){
  instructions
}
```

This is another example of how the C for loop can be used in ways that aren't obvious from its simpler form. In this case there is no initialization and no increment expressions. The loop simply continues while the *condition* is true and if nothing in the *instructions* changes the *condition* it loops forever.

Do ... while

There is a variant on the while loop that is worth knowing about - the do-while loop. Its most basic form is:

```
do instruction; while (condition);
```

This repeats the instruction while the condition is true. However, the order of the test is slightly different. The instruction is obeyed first and then the condition evaluated, if it is true the instruction is obeyed again and the condition evaluated and so on..

Of course the more common form of the do-while loop makes use of a compound statement to repeat a block of code:

```
do {
  instruction1;
  instruction2;
  instruction3;
} while(condition);
```

Again the block of code is obeyed while the condition is true. To see why this variant on the while loop is needed consider what the minimum number of times a while loop can be carried out. For example:

```
a=10
while(a<10){
 instructions;
}
```

In this case, because a isn't less than 10 when the loop starts, the body of the loop isn't carried out at all, i.e. it is skipped.

Compare this to:

```
a=10;
do{
 instructions;
} while(a<10);
```

In this case the test that ends the loop comes at the end of the loop. What this means is that the instructions in the loop will be obeyed at least once.

This is the only difference between the while and the do-while loops - the test is either at the start or the end of the loop respectively. This in turn means that the while loop can skip over the loop and so the minimum number of repeats is zero. In contrast, the do-while loop has to execute at least one repeat. That is, a for and while loop repeat zero or more times but a do-while loop repeats one or more times.

You will quickly learn which form of the loop you need even if it seems a bit confusing at first. If you need to do something once before the condition can be tested than you need a do-while, otherwise you probably need a while.

Flow of Control in Practice

Flow of control is the difficult part of learning to program. You now should understand the ideas that are behind it, but you might be unsure how to use them. The only cure for this is to practice. There is nothing more to know but you need to put theory into practice. It is a bit like just learning where the notes are on a piano - you next need to practice some scales before moving on to a sonata. So we need some examples.

At this stage it isn't easy to invent realistic examples of how to use control statements without introducing a lot more C. However, to close without seeing some real code in action isn't satisfying. So let's write a simple program that demonstrates the if, if else, for, while and do while loops. These aren't realistic or convincing but they are simple. Enter the code and try it out. Modify it and see if you are happy with the result.

If you are a complete beginner to programming, absorbing the way that control statements work is hard, but once you have done it learning the rest of programming is easy.

Start a new C project. We are going to enter some simple code snippets into the main program and see what they do.

if

First we look at a simple if statement:

```
int total = 100;
if (total == 100) {
 printf("total= %d\n\r", total);
}
```

The command `printf` stands for "print formatted" and it will print the value of the integer variable total in the Output window which you can see in NetBeans' default layout just below the source listing. Don't worry too much about `printf` for the moment - it will occupy enough of your future C life as a way to get simple output.

If you type in and run the above what do you expect to see?

Answer: you should see `100` printed in the Output window. Now change total to be 99. Now you should see nothing at all printed.

if else

An if ..else is fairly easy:

```
if (total == 100) {
  printf("value is 100");
} else {
  printf("value is not 100");
}
```

When you run this you will see "`value is 100`" printed.

What do you see if you change the value of total to 99?

You will see just the message "`value is not 100`". Notice you only ever see one of the two messages.

for

In the case of the for loop:

```
for (int i = 1; i <= 10; i++) {
  printf("%d\n\r", i);
}
```

what do you expect to see printed? Be exact.

The answer is 1 to 10 because each time through the loop i increases by 1 until it reaches 11 when the loop ends without executing the body of the loop again i.e. with the value of i set to 11.

Notice that this needs at least C99 because of the way the loop counter i is declared within the loop. If you want to use earlier versions of C you would have to declare the variable before the loop.

As an aside, there is a long history of using i, j and k as counters in loops - the reason is that i is the first letter of integer and a counter or index in a for loop is always an integer. It was a convention started with the language Fortran. Today programmers still tend to use i, j and k as loop counters, but it would be better to use a meaningful name.

while

Consider a real situation where only the while loop will do, even if it is contrived. How many times can a number be divided by two before it is less than or equal to one? We can simulate this by writing a while loop that divides the given number and tests for it being greater than one:

```
int number = 10;
while (number > 1) {
 printf("%d\n\r", number);
 number = number / 2;
}
```

This is should be easy enough for you to follow. The statement says take the contents of number, divide it by 2 and store the result back in the variable number. If you run the program you will see it print 5 and 2 as after the 2 is printed the value is divided by 2 again with the result 1 and the loop ends.

Notice that as number is an int it has no fractional part and so division is integer division where any remainder or fractional part is ignored. That is in integer arithmetic 5/2 is 2 not 2.5 or 2 remainder 1.

You can do the same job with a do-while loop:

```
number = 10;
do {
  printf("%d\n\r", number);
  number = number / 2;
} while (number > 1);
```

The difference is that now the test is done at the end of the loop. It is arguable that in this case the test being at the end makes it easier to see why and when the loop comes to an end. However, the real difference between the two is that if you set number to one and run each loop the while loop prints nothing at all but the do-while loop prints one; it's all a matter of where the test to end the loop is performed.

Also notice the way indents are used to show where blocks of code start and end. The content of an if, else, for, while and do-while should be indented.

Fractional Loops – Break and Continue

C loops are simple and cover most of the things you need to do. They all repeat a block of code, the body of the loop, a number of times. The loop exits at the start of the body – the for loop and the do-while loop – or at the end of the loop – the while loop. These forms of loop are more than you need to write any program but there are times when a problem is easier to solve by jumping out of a loop in the middle of the block of code rather than just at the start or the end. You can do this using the break statement.

At its simplest, break brings a loop to an end.

For example:

```
while(x>0){
  do something 1;
 if(condition) break;
  do something 2;
}
```

In this case the loop will exit when the if statement's condition is true. When the loop exits via the break, the instructions before the break will have been executed once more than the instructions after the break, i.e do something 1 will execute one more time than do something 2. In this sense the break lets you write loops that execute a fractional number of time – e.g. the loop repeats two and a half times. This isn't how you generally think of using a break statement, however. Typically what happens is that you need to write a for loop that is used to search for something. If you don't find it then the for loop ends normally but if you do find it then you can use a break to jump out of the loop and so avoid continuing the search when the thing you are looking for has been found. The break statement works with all three of C's loops – for, while and do-while.

The `continue` statement works like `break`, but it causes the loop to abandon the current iteration and start over at the test of the condition. If the break statement is like a jump out of the loop to the instruction following, the continue is like a jump to the start of the next iteration. Notice that for the for and while loops the jump is back to the start of the loop but for the do-while it is to the end of the loop where the conditional test is.

For example:
```
while(x>0){
   do something 1;
  if(condition) continue;
   do something 2;
}
```
In this case the loop moves on to the next iteration if the condition is true. This means that *do something 1* might be executed any number of times more often than *do something 2*. In fact, if the condition is always true, *do something 2* never gets executed. The continue statement works with all three of C's loops – for, while and do- while.

Both break and continue in loops are unnecessary in the sense you can always write something equivalent without them. Some are of the opinion that they should never be used and that loops should always end at the start or the beginning of the body, as this is what most programmers expect, and exits in the middle of a loop can be easily overlooked. A more moderate attitude is to only use break and continue when they provide a significant simplification and where the resulting code is arguably clearer than without their use.

Nesting

Once you have the basics of the default flow of control, conditionals and loops, you can start to work on putting them together like basic building bricks used to create more complex things. In general there are only two ways to put these building bricks together. You can put one after the other so you could have a conditional followed by a loop followed by a conditional. The second, more complicated, way is to put one structure inside another - nesting them. So you can have a loop inside a conditional inside a loop etc. For example, suppose you want to print a message to say a number is odd or even, you might use something like:
```
for (int i = 1; i <= 10; i++) {
   if (i / 2 * 2 == i) {
      printf("even\n\r");
   } else {
      printf("odd\n\r");
   }
}
```

You can see that there is a for loop and within it is an if statement. The if statement is nested within the for loop and so repeated ten times. The only "tricky" part of the program is the condition within the if statement. If you take an integer like 7 and divide it by 2 the result isn't a fraction, but the exact number of times 2 goes into 7, i.e. 3. This is integer division. When you multiply this by 2 you get 6, which is not equal to 7, and odd is printed.

If you repeat the procedure using an even number like 8 you get 8/2 is 4 and 4*2 is 8 which is equal to 8 and so the program prints even. Integer division may not be accurate, but it is often very useful in programming. In general, if a number x is even then x/2*2 is equal to x, but if it is odd then it is smaller than x - try it.

The more control statements you nest the more complicated the program becomes and this is a bad thing. Over the years, we have found ways of avoiding building complicated structures like this. In particular, you can often hide nested structures by defining functions, which is the topic of Chapter 7.

For now, simply make sure you understand the conditional and the loop; you will see both used a lot in following chapters.

The Switch Statement

Sometimes you want to conditionally select what happens based on a complicated set of conditions and this usually leads to a set of nested ifs. Take a simple situation with three products 0, 1 and 2. For 0 the discount is 10; for 1 costing less than $100 the discount is 5 and 8 otherwise; and for 2 the discount is 2. All other products have zero discount.

Let's implement a nested if for this:

```
if (product == 0) {
    discount = 10;
} else if (product == 1) {
    if (cost < 100) {
        discount = 5;
    } else {
        discount = 8;
    }
} else if (product == 2) {
    discount = 2;
} else {
    discount = 0;
}
```

Good luck with pairing up the brackets. I'm not claiming that this is the best way to nest conditions, just that it is typical.

Notice that as an else takes a single statement, you don't need brackets to following it by an else. That is, you can write:

```
}else if(..){
```

rather than:

```
}else { if(..){
```

Nested ifs quickly become too complicated to be sure that they are correct. In situations where the conditions are constants, like product 0, 1 or 2 then we can use the C switch statement, which is much simpler – if not altogether error proof.

The switch statement takes the form:

```
switch(variable)
{
    case constant1:
        instructions;
        break;
    case constant2:
        instructions;
        break;
    case constant3:
        instructions;
        break;
.   .   .
  default:
        instructions;
}
```

The variable and the constants have to be integer types and notice the colon after each line starting case.

What happens is that the case statement with the constant that matches the contents of the variable is carried out. That is the variable picks out which of the cases is executed depending on its value.

The break statement is optional and it takes the flow of control out of the switch. If you leave the break out then the case statements following the selected case statement are executed. This is often expressed by saying that control "falls through" the switch statement if you don't include break within each case.

This is usually not what you want and it is the source of many difficult to find errors.

For an example with break statements:

```
switch (state) {
    case 0:
        printf("zero");
        break;
    case 1:
        printf("one");
        break;
    case 2:
        printf("two");
        break;
    default:
        printf("out of range");
}
```

If state is 0, 1 or 2 you will see the appropriate message printed. If it is any other value then the default is taken and you see out of range printed. Notice that only one of the cases, including default, is executed. If you leave out a break then control passes to the next case and so on.

For an extreme example of leaving out break statements consider:

```
switch (state) {
    case 0:
        printf("zero");
    case 1:
        printf("one");
    case 2:
        printf("two");
    default:
        printf("out of range");
}
```

Now if state is 1, you will see one, two, out of range printed. This sort of construct is sometimes useful, but as it is not what the average programmer expects it is dangerous.

While break statements are sometimes correctly left out of some of the cases it is much more usual to simply forget to include a break in a case which causes it to fall through to the next case. This often occurs when code is being copied and pasted from one program to another. What makes it worse is if the case containing the error is only selected infrequently this can be a very difficult bug to find as it makes it look as if the state variable must be is occasionally wrong for no good reason.

If a program containing a switch starts to misbehave then it is always worth checking that the breaks are where you expect them to be before moving to full debugging mode.

Finally, here is the nested if example implemented as a switch:

```
switch (product) {
    case 0:
        discount = 10;
        break;
    case 1:
        if (cost < 100) {
            discount = 5;
        } else {
            discount = 8;
        }
        break;
    case 2:
        discount = 2;
        break;
    default:
        discount = 0;
}
```

It is simpler, easier to understand and hence less error prone, as long as you don't forget any of the breaks. Notice that the inner if statement cannot be replaced by a switch.

A common idiom in physical computing is the use of a switch to implement a state machine.

Consider a small computer controlling a device that can be on, active, idle or off. If you represent these states by 0, 1, 2, 3 you can write a switch that responds to each state and then changes the state accordingly. So on might go to active, then to idle and so on. Each state corresponds to a case and each case sets the variable to determine the next state.

Summary

- Variables are the basic way of storing and working with data in a program.

- C programs have a main function which is where they start executing.

- The flow of control is a key idea in programming. There are only three fundamental forms – default, conditional and looping.

- The conditional in C takes the form of the if statement and the if else statement.

- Grouping instructions together in parentheses results in C treating them as a single compound instruction.

- There are two distinct types of loop – enumeration and conditional.

- The C for loop is particularly complicated because it follows the way all loops are constructed in assembly language.

- The goto instruction is the C analog of the assembler jump instruction and it can be used to make all of the standard forms of flow of control.

- There are also two conditional loops – the while loop and the do-while loop.

- The for and while loop can repeat zero or more times whereas the do-while loop always executes once.

- The three standard loops always exit from the start or end of the body but you can use break and continue to jump out of a loop early or skip part of the body.

- The simpler flow of control constructs can be nested inside each other to produce more complex structures.

- Nested ifs are particularly difficult to work with and C provides the switch statement as an easier alternative.

Chapter 4

Variables

Data is often under-regarded by programmers. It just isn't as exciting as writing the code that does something with that data. In fact nothing could be further from the truth and C in particular is a language that was designed to have data at its core - but not for the same reasons that most modern languages do.

One of the big differences between a language like C and more abstract languages like Java or C# is that C was designed to be close to the way that the machine works in terms of data. C creates abstract constructs that make writing code easier than writing in assembler. It gives you for and while loops, if statements and so on, which are much simpler to use than the lower level sequences of assembly language needed to do the same tasks.

When it comes to data, however, C stays very close to the addressing and the organization of RAM that you find in a real machine. This is a big plus point if you are looking to make effective use of memory. It is also essential if you are writing code which interacts with hardware that is represented as particular areas of memory. The problem is this flexibility and realism entails some major responsibilities. It is up to you to organize and use memory in sensible ways. It is all too easy to write programs that stray into areas of memory they were never intended to access. This is the reason why C code has a reputation for being buggy and dangerous. It is undeniably low-level code and as such the only way to write safe, high-quality code is to understand how C works and know what it is you are trying to achieve.

Being so close to the hardware means you can write programs that work with it in ways that other languages make difficult. You also learn how the hardware works and this is a valuable education in itself.

Finally, C is low-level in another sense. What is stored in memory is best regarded as a pattern of bits rather than a particular type of data. In C programming you often will treat an area of memory as an int and later on treat it as a character or an int of a different size. What matters in C is the bit pattern, and we will investigate this further in much of the rest of this book.

Memory Basics

Computer memory is organized into chunks of storage which are fixed in size, typically 16 or 32 bits. Generally each chunk of storage has a unique address which is used to identify it. It is also usual that parts of a chunk of storage will also have addresses. For example most modern machines assign an address to the individual bytes that makeup a larger memory unit.

Back in the days when C was being invented, the standard machine of the day, the PDP 11, organized its memory as 16-bit words. This means that if you specified an address, you read or wrote a single 16-bit word. When C was created its fundamental data type was int and this was assumed to be a 16-bit or2-byte storage location.

So what is the size of an int today?

The answer might surprise you. It is still decided by the compiler implemented for the machine. Many C programmers believe that C data types have a fixed size; they don't, and they vary according to the machine you are using.

This might seem like madness if you are familiar with other higher level languages, but C is designed to be close to the machine it is running on. When you say you want to use an int, you are asking for a variable that is the fundamental access unit of the machine. That is, reading or writing the variable involves one memory access. For example, suppose the C standard defined int to be 32-bits in size and you were working on a machine that had a memory organized into 16-bit words. Now when you stored or retrieved something from an int, 32 bits would have to be transferred and this would mean two memory accesses on a machine with a 16-bit word. This would slow your programs down significantly.

The way C actually operates means that when you ask for an int variable you get a word size that corresponds to the most efficient memory access the machine can offer.

Of course, even this rule is likely to be broken because it is up to the compiler writer to implement whatever makes sense in the circumstances, but this is the intent. The same is also true of the other data types and this is the reason that their sizes are not fixed.

The vagueness about int extends beyond its size. An int should be capable of holding a signed value, i.e. both positive and negative values, but the format used to store this isn't specified. There are two common ways to represent negative numbers, one's complement and two's complement. Most common hardware uses two's complement and this is usually what you encounter in a C int, but it isn't mandated. Even so, many programmers think that when they declare an int they get a 2- or 4-byte memory location holding a two's-complement value, but this doesn't have to be so. An `int` should be the natural size for the machine in use and the numeric format is whatever the machine uses when it does arithmetic. All in all this is very vague.

So how do C programmers cope with this vagueness? Sometimes it doesn't matter because the program would work with a 2-byte int and just as well with a 4-byte int and the numeric representation doesn't matter. Sometimes it does matter and in these cases you need to use data types that are guaranteed to be particular sizes - more of this later.

The often overlooked fact is that C is a language that targets specific machines and if you want to know what the data types are you have to ask what the target machine is. For nearly all machines with a 16-bit architecture, a C int is a two's-complement 16-bit value; for 32-bit architectures int is a two's-complement 32-bit value. However, for a machine with a 64-bit architecture int is still usually 32 bits because this is more efficient than using 64-bit integers.

The Numeric Data Types

C only has two fundamental data types – integer and floating point. Everything else is constructed using these two. Integer types, as the name suggests, store integer values, i.e. no decimal fractions are stored.

C has a range of integer data types, but how they are implemented depends, just like the basic `int`, on the architecture of the machine. However, the most commonly encountered sizes are:

char	1 byte	-128 to 127 or 0 to 255
short	2 bytes	-32,768 to 32,767
int	2 or 4 bytes	-32,768 to 32,767 or -2,147,483,648 to 2,147,483,647
long	4 bytes	-2,147,483,648 to 2,147,483,647
long long	8 bytes	−9223372036854775808 to +9223372036854775807

The `long long` type was defined in C99.

The char type is often assumed to be exactly 1 byte, but this is just its most common implementation. The reason it is called char is that it has to be capable of storing the basic character set codes of the machine. Notice that it can be a signed value or an unsigned value, again this depends on the machine. If you want to be certain that char is signed you can use the qualifier `signed` in front of `char` to give `signed char`. If you want the values stored in a variable to be unsigned, i.e. just positive integers, you can use the qualifier `unsigned` in front of the type. For example, `unsigned char`, means a single byte can store values in the range 0 to 255.

There is one final complication. You can put int after any of the length qualifiers. So a short can be declared as short int, a long as long int and a long long as long long int. This is mostly a matter of preference. Many C programmers prefer the shortest form of a declaration so instead of long long int they would use long long.

Notice that while most implementations of C have these data types, it might not be wise to make use of them if they are not efficiently supported by the hardware. For example the ARM 11 architecture is 32-bit and hence short actually uses as much storage as an int and takes longer to do arithmetic. It is not necessarily true that smaller is better.

The char Type

The char type is a little different in that, while it is an 8-bit integer value, it is intended to be used to store basic character codes. When C was first designed the characters were most often represented by the 7-bit ASCII code. A char data type was able to store an ASCII character code and to make this easier you could assign an ASCII literal – a single character in single quotes. Things still work this way, for example:

```
char myChar='A';
```

has the same effect as:

```
char myChar=65;
```

as the ASCII code for A is 65 decimal.

Even though char looks as if it might be exclusively a character type, it is a perfectly usable integer type. You can do arithmetic with a char variable. For example:

```
char myChar='A';
myChar=myChar+1;
```

sets myChar to 66 which is the ASCII code for B.

You can use character literals with other integer types and this is occasionally useful. For example:

```
int myInteger:
myInteger='A';
```

sets myInteger to 65. It is sometimes useful to know that a character literal is treated as if it was an int.

Today Unicode has replaced ASCII but the first 128 characters of Unicode are the same as the ASCII characters. You can regard character literals as UTF-8 encodings of the first 128 Unicode characters. Using the full Unicode range of characters in C is not easy – see Chapter 9.

Working With Boolean values

Most computer languages have a special data type generally called `bool` or `boolean` to hold the special values `true` and `false`. C doesn't have a Boolean type. Instead, when an integer type is used to represent true or false, a zero value is taken to be `false` and any other value is `true`.

When you use a comparison operator, in an `if` statement say, then the result is 1 for true and 0 for false. You can also use comparisons outside of `if` statements, for example:

```
int myInteger;
myInteger= (1>3);
```

sets `myInteger` to 0 and:

```
myInteger=(3>1);
```

sets `myInteger` to 1.

The lack of a Boolean type has troubled C programmers for a long time and in C89 you will often find that an enumerated type, see Chapter 8, is used to simulate the availability of variables that work with true and false. In C99 this was formalized in an additional library file. If you add:

```
#include stdbool.h
```

to the start of a program you can declare a variable to be `bool` and use `true` and `false`:

```
bool myInteger;
myInteger= true;
```

However, nothing is changed in the way things work and `true` is 1, `false` is 0 and `bool` variables are just integers and can be used anywhere an `int` can.

Floating Point

The second fundamental data type is the floating-point value. This is a numeric value with a fractional part – even if that fractional part happens to be zero.

As with integer types, C pays attention to the hardware that is available in its implementation of floating-point numbers. So much so that the basic `float` is whatever the hardware offers. Things are, however, more standardized than you might imagine because in practice most hardware implements the IEEE 754 standard for single-precision binary floating-point arithmetic. This means that in C `float` is a 4-byte, 32-bit single-precision floating-point value in the range -3.4E38 .. 3.4E38 with between 6 and 9 digits of precision. This is also the standard adopted by C99.

For higher precision there is the `double` data type, which is generally implemented as an IEEE 754 double-precision floating-point number. This means that in C `double` is an 8-byte, 64-bit floating-point value in the range -1.7E308 .. 1.7E308 with between 15 and 17 digits of precision.

There is also a `long double` type which is much more varied in its implementation and often not implemented at all. Typically, long double is mapped to the IEEE 80-bit, extended-precision type, but there are also machines where it is mapped to a 128-bit floating-point value.

It is worth knowing that many small CPUs don't have floating point in hardware and in this case you either cannot use floating-point types or you have to use a software implementation, which is very slow. In such situations, it is usually possible to avoid the need for floating point by implementing arithmetic using a fixed-point scheme.

Using floating point is very easy, perhaps too easy. You can specify numbers and operations without thinking about what is happening and then just get the results. However they aren't always the correct results. Sometimes floating point calculations can be very inaccurate.

All of this is covered in detail in:

Applying C For The IoT With Linux ISBN: 978-1871962611.

Complex Numbers

Although not commonly used in low-level C code, C99 supports complex numbers and functions. To use them you need to include the `complex.h` header and following this you can declare a complex version of any floating-point type:

```
#include <complex.h>

double complex z1 = 1.0 + 3.0 * I;
```

Notice that `I` is set to the square root of `-1`. If you want to use some other letter you can change this. You can use the standard arithmetic operators with complex types and they perform complex arithmetic. There is also a full range of complex functions that you can use. These are generally have the same name as the standard function but with a `c` added. For example, `csin` and `ccos` are the complex versions of `sin` and `cos`. You can also use `carg` for the argument and `cconj` for the complex conjugate. If you want to print a complex value then you have to use `creal` and `cimag` to print the real and imaginary parts separately.

If you know about complex numbers you should have no problem using C's implementation. You can find more information in the header file and the manual.

Declaring Variables

Before you can use a variable you have to declare it as being of a fixed type. This idea was introduced in earlier chapters. Declaring a variable lets the compiler know what it is called and how much memory to set aside for it. It also tells the compiler how to implement operations that involve the variable.

For example:

```
int myinteger;
```

creates a variable that is suitable for storing an integer and if you use `myinteger` in an arithmetic expression the compiler knows that it has to use integer operations.

You can declare multiple variables of the same type in one statement. For example:

```
int myinteger1, myinteger2, myinteger3;
```

and each of the variables are ints.

Notice that, unlike other languages, C doesn't make a strong distinction between data types – it really only recognizes integer types and floating-point types. For example, you might think that the type `char` is some how different to `int`, but `char` is just a small `int` capable of holding a character code - you can still do integer arithmetic with it. That is, for all integer types, arithmetic means integer arithmetic and for floating-point types it means floating-point arithmetic. For low-level programming this simple approach is a big advantage, even if it can be a source of bugs if you are not aware of the problems.

Notice that you have to declare a variable before you use it. The reason is that if you were allowed to declare a variable after its use, as you can in many languages, the compiler would have to scan your code at least twice – once to gather the declarations and a second time to make sense of them. The C compiler is generally designed to be a one-pass compiler and therefore it is up to you to put your declarations first. This generally means that C programmers gather their declarations to be at the start of the program. This isn't a hard and fast rule, however, and some programmers follow the convention of declaring variables where they are first used.

Also notice that variable names are case sensitive and, even though you can write long variable names, only the first 31 characters are used by the compiler. There are also special characters that you can't use in a name and you cannot use any of the names that have special meaning in C such as int. In most cases it is easier to just let the compiler tell you that you have constructed an illegal name than to worry about the rules.

Initialization

We now come to the question of initialization. This is one of the many things that causes some programmers to consider C dangerous.

What does a variable contain when you declare it?

Often the answer is whatever was in the memory that is used to store it. C doesn't do anything that isn't essential to make sure that you can write a fast and efficient program.

When you write:

```
int myVariable;
```

the compiler simply sets myVariable as a reference to some area of memory.

When the program is run, nothing is done to initialize the memory location and this means there are no overheads at all. Of course, if you use the variable without storing something in it, the result is that you will find whatever was stored in the memory before. This is why it is dangerous - uninitialized variables can cause very difficult-to-find bugs.

As explained later, the system will initialize to zero all global and static variables for you. For example, if you try:

```
int i;
printf("%d",i);
```

you will see a value printed that is the bit pattern of whatever was stored in the memory location before the variable was allocated, interpreted as an integer. If you try this out and see 0 printed then the compiler is doing more work for you that in needs to, according to the specification. Notice that this opens up the possibility that you could read data left by another program. This is a technique that is used by malware to read leaked data, but hardware has evolved various memory scrambling techniques to stop this happening.

You can initialize a variable by storing something in it:

```
int myVariable;
myVariable=0;
```

which does give your program something to do when it is first loaded i.e. myVariable=0 is an instruction that has to be carried out.

As an alternative you can use an initialization:

```
int myVariable=0;
```

Notice that the two approaches are usually implemented in different ways. The separate assignment often causes the compiler to issue an assembly language statement that moves zero into the variable at run time. The combined declaration and assignment generally cause the compiler to simply initialize the new variable to zero as part of the loading of your program with no assignment instructions carried out at runtime.

You can also initialize multiple variables in a single statement:

```
int myVariable1=0, myVariable2=42, myVariable3=3;
```

In general you should initialize variables unless you have a really good reason not to. One of the best reasons for not initializing variable is that it would involve writing out a lot of explicit values. This becomes particularly important when we start using arrays.

Using a variable that hasn't been initialized isn't, as is often claimed, "undefined behavior" unless that variable is of register storage class, as will soon be explained.

Literals

If you are going to initialize variables you have to know how to write values that are suitable. C has a range of ways of letting you specify a value and its type. For integers you can write in decimal, octal or hexadecimal.

An octal constant is signified by a leading 0 - so don't write unnecessary leading zeros on decimal literals. Hex literals are much safer because they start with 0x, which isn't likely to be entered by accident. The use of 0x to mean hex has more or less become standard across many languages.

So 77 is 77 in decimal but 077 is 63 in octal and 0xFF is 255 in hex. There is more about hex in Chapter 5.

A floating-point literal is signified by having a decimal point - 1 is an integer and 1.0 is a float.

You can also write an exponent as in 1E3 which is a float with the value 1000, i.e. 1 followed by an exponent of 10^3 i.e. 1*1000.

You can also use a suffix to specify the type of a literal:

- ◆ 1.0f is a float
- ◆ 2u is an unsigned int
- ◆ 3L is a long
- ◆ 4Lu is an unsigned long
- ◆ 5LL is a long long
- ◆ 6LLu is an unsigned long long.

Often the compiler will work out what the literal should be without any help from you.

For example, there is no suffix for a short literal because the compiler simply attempts to fit the int literal into the short variable and, if it fits, it doesn't complain. When you write a literal the compiler tries to fit it into an int, if it doesn't fit it tries a long and then a long long.

Most of the time you don't have to specify a type for a literal, but sometimes it is essential to avoid a compiler error. For example, if you try:

```
long long y = 2147483647 * 100;
```

you will most likely find that y is -100, which is not the answer you were expecting. If this happens the reason is that the literals are treated as ints as they are within the range of a 4-byte int, but the arithmetic performed using the literals overflows and this erroneous result is stored in y. In other words the literals are evaluated as 4-byte ints and overflow even though the assignment is to a variable that is large enough to store the exact result.

The solution is to explicitly set the constants to LL:

```
long long y = 2147483647LL * 100LL;
```

which now gives the correct result.

Implementing Variables

We work with variables all the time and we think we know what a variable is, but how languages implement variables is one of the big differences between them. C takes the most basic approach possible, one that, as you might expect, is close to the way the machine does things.

When you declare a variable the right amount of memory is allocated for it somewhere – exactly where is discussed in Chapter 10. That area of memory has an address and its address is used in all the assembly language instructions that the compiler generates that need to work with that variable. Consider the simple program:

```
int i;
i=0;
```

When the compiler processes this, it generates:

```
! i=0;
main+11: movl    $0x0,0x407020
```

The movl (move long) instruction stores the value $0x0, i.e. 0, in address 0x407020. You can see that the variable is reduced to the address and there is no sign of anything called i in the assembler that is generated. The declaration of i did not generate any assembler. It simply told the compiler that it should allocate some memory and use its address anywhere that i is used in the program.

What happens is that when the compiler encounters a variable declaration it stores the variables name in an internal table – the symbol table. It then allocates some memory for the variable and stores the address in the symbol table along with the variable name. From this point on if you use the variable name the symbol table is used to look the name up and retrieve the address which is then used in the assembler being generated. When the compiler has finished the symbol table is deleted – it is not part of your program and hence the names of all of the variables are not part of your program. The exception is when you make use of a debugger. In this case the compiler passes the symbol table to the debugger and it uses it to convert the addresses used in your program to the names of variable. In this way you can carry on in the belief that your program uses named variables.

Although we haven't met the idea of pointers as yet, it is worth explaining now that this is an example of a constant pointer. You can think of the address as a pointer to an area of storage and in this sense a variable is a constant pointer, i.e. a pointer that never changes. The value of the constant pointer is used within the assembly language program wherever it is needed.

Exact Size Variables

Most of the time you can work with C's strange approach to variable types because you are targeting a particular machine.

The solution to the problem of how to work with variables that have a definite number of bits is to use the `stdint.h` header file. This is a library that was introduced in C99 to provide a set of types that are fixed in size, irrespective of the machine in use. Of course, the implementation might not be the most efficient possible on the machine.

The library introduces new types of the form:

```
intN_t
uintN_t
```

for signed and unsigned integers with N bits. The only values of N that have to be implemented in the library are 8, 16, 32 and 64. The signed types are implemented as two's complement. Note that the implementations have to be exact and no padding bits are allowed.

To use the library you have to add:

```
#include <stdint.h>
```

to the other automatically generated includes in your program. So, for example:

```
int8_t just8bits;
```

is guaranteed to be an 8-bit variable and:

```
uint16_t just2bytes;
```

is guaranteed to be a two-byte unsigned int.

This all works well, but if the machine doesn't support `int16_t` as a native two-byte int the results could be very slow. There is an alternative which lets you specify either the minimum width that can be used:

```
int_leastN_t
```

or:

```
uint_leastN_t
```

or the fastest minimum width:

```
int_fastN_t
```

or:

```
uint_fastN_t.
```

For example:

```
int_least8_t mybyte;
```

will create a variable that is as small as possible, but still greater than or equal to 8 bits. The fast version gives you a variable that is as small as possible, but with the extra condition that it is fast. So, for example:

```
int_fast8_t mybyte;
```

will be at least 8 bits, but it might be larger if it is faster to use a bigger variable type. Exactly how these are implemented is left up to the compiler writer.

In practice using `stdint.h` is a good idea, even if you are targeting a fixed machine, because it makes clear the exact size of the variables that are in use. Specifically, if you write:

```
int myvar;
```

then a programmer unfamiliar with the machine is left wondering what the size of the variable is, but if you use:

```
int16_t myvar;
```

then, even though this might map to int, it makes it clear that this is a 16-bit int.

There are also macros that will create literals in the correct type:

```
INTN_C(value)
UINTN_C(value)
```

create signed and unsigned literals with N bits. For example:

```
INT16_C(255)
```

creates a 16-bit signed constant for 255.

There is more to say about macros in Chapter 14.

Type Modifiers

There are three type modifiers that you need to know about, `const`, `volatile` and `register`. Of the three `const` is really only useful after you have learned about pointers and arguably `register` is mostly useless.

You can add the type modifier `const` to any declaration. For example:

```
const int myvar=42;
```

declares `myvar` to be constant. This means you can't assign to it. Clearly you have to initialize a const, because how else would it get a value. There are some subtleties about const that only become apparent later. Notice that `myvar` is still an allocated variable that is implemented in the usual way, it's just the compiler stops you from changing its value. Later we'll cover another way to create "real" constants using the preprocessor – see Chapter 14.

The second type modifier is `volatile`. This sometimes is introduced as being the opposite of `const` but this isn't exactly the case. A `volatile` variable is one who's value can change because of external actions. That is, if you read a volatile variable and then read it a second time without assigning to it, you can still get two different values. Typically a `volatile` variable corresponds to some hardware register or memory location that is being changed by the hardware. You need to declare such a variable as `volatile` to stop the compiler from assuming that it doesn't change between reads. For example:

```
int time;
a = time;
do something else that doesn't assign to time;
a = time;
```

In this case the compiler could well remove the second a=time instruction on the grounds that time cannot have changed. To make sure that this doesn't happen time has to be declared as:

```
volatile int time;
```

A very common use of volatile is to make sure a null `for` loop isn't optimized away. That is:

```
for(volatile int i; i<100; i++){};
```

is usually not removed by an optimizing compiler but without the `volatile` it often is silently removed leaving the programmer wondering why the timing loop isn't slowing the program down.

The final qualifier that we need to consider - `register` is a hint to the compiler that the variable is best held in a register rather than in memory. As register optimization is a complex business best handled by the compiler the `register` qualifier is mostly ignored by modern compilers. However, you cannot take the address of a `register` variable – it doesn't have an address as it is stored in a register and not in memory and you have to initialize it. This can be useful even if the compiler ignores the qualifier and doesn't place the variable in a register.

Variable Lifetimes

In general, you also have to inquire about the rules for how long a variable exists in any language. So far variables declared inside the main function are available to the program for the lifetime of the program. Later we will find that the behavior is more complicated than this, but to see the full picture we need to ask how variables are affected by being declared in other functions and so this topic is best left to Chapter 7. There is also the question of where a variable can be used within a program and this is generally referred to as its scope. This too is best left to Chapter 7.

lvalue and rvalue

It is clear that in an assignment there are left- and right-hand sides. Consider:

```
a=2;
```

In this case `a` is called an lvalue and `2` is called an rvalue. There is an important distinction between these two types of thing. The lvalue is the address of a modifiable entity. The rvalue is something that has a value, but it doesn't have an address that can be used to access it. What this means is that:

```
2=a;
```

is nonsense – you can't assign to `2` as it doesn't have an address that you can work with.

However, notice that you can write:

```
b=a;
```

so lvalue doesn't mean strictly on the left-hand side. Today we generally say that an lvalue is a locator value and it can be assigned to or retrieved and hence it can be used on both sides of an assignment.

By contrast an rvalue really can only be used on the right of an assignment – it is, or can be reduced to, a value.

As a more subtle point, you could argue that 2 is a literal and has to be stored somewhere and so modifying the literal is possible and so perhaps an rvalue can be assigned to. This is sometimes the case, but what about 2*b+a? This is an expression and while its constituents are stored somewhere its effective value is computed when needed. This is an rvalue for which assignment makes no sense and the simple literal 2 is a special case of an expression.

The idea of an lvalue that has an "address" and an rvalue that might well not have an address is often helpful in understanding why some things can't be used where an address is required.

Summary

- C has only two basic types of data – integer and floating-point.

- The amount of memory that a data type takes is machine-dependent.

- Variables have to be declared before use and optionally initialized.

- All integer types come in signed and unsigned forms.

- C doesn't have Boolean type which stores true and false. Instead integer types are used with 0 as false and any other value as false.

- C99 adds a boolean type which uses 0 as false and 1 as true. Before C99 programmer invented a number of ways of making it seem as if there was a true and false value.

- C99 also added a complex type which is implemented as a pair of floating-point types.

- Character literals can be used to store ASCII or UTF-8 character codes in an integer type.

- It is a good idea to specify the type of any literal you are using.

- Variables can be regarded as constant pointers. There is no trace of a variable's name in the assembler that the compiler produces just the address that it was assigned.

- You can use integer types that have a well defined size via the stdint.h library introduced in C99.

- Variables can be declared as const to make sure they cannot be changed and volatile to make sure that the compiler cannot assume that they do not change.

- How long a variable exists and where you can use it – lifetime and scope – are important ideas but they only make sense when you have understood functions in a later chapter.

- C makes use of the idea of an lvalue, something that has an address, and an rvalue, something that doesn't.

Chapter 5

Arithmetic and Representation

A key idea in using C is that what is stored in a variable is a bit pattern and what it means is up to how you process it. In this chapter we look at the most fundamental representation - simple binary integers. This is enough for many applications, but sooner or later you are going to need negative integers as well. What is surprising is that the change from `unsigned int` to `int` is just a matter of changing how you interpret the bit patterns.

Positive Integers

A set of bits most naturally represents a positive integer. You probably are already familiar with binary but it is worth remembering that it is just counting in base 2. The first bit, usually denoted as bit 0, or the least significant bit, represents 0 or 1. The next bit represents 0 or 2, the next 0 or 4 and so on. The last bit you use has the highest value and is generally called the most significant bit. As bit patterns are stored in variables of a fixed size, i.e. a fixed number of bits, there is always a most significant bit which can be zero or one. For example, for a char variable which can hold eight bits the most significant bit is bit 7.

To convert a binary number to decimal you simply add up all the powers of two. For example, 1110 in decimal is:

`1*8 + 1*4 + 1*2 + 0*1 = 14`

Converting from decimal to binary is just a matter of finding out how many lots of each power of two there are in a given number. For example, to convert 14 to binary you first notice that there is one lot of 8 which leaves 6, which in turn has one lot of 4 with 2 left over, giving:

`14=8+4+2`

or:

`1110`

Notice that you can read any bit pattern as if it was a positive integer. For example, if the bit pattern 1110 corresponds to the state of three lights – light 3 on, light 2 on, light 1 on and light 0 off – you can still read the bit pattern as 14.

Hexadecimal

We have already had occasion to use hexadecimal notation – assembly language uses it by default. Hexadecimal counts in lots of 16, just as decimal counts in lots of 10 and binary lots of 2. To count a single lot of 16 needs 16 symbols and these are usually taken to be 0,1..9, A, B, C, D, E, F. That is, A is 10, B is 11 and so on to F which is 15. Once you get to 15+1 you need another symbol to represent one lot of 16, i.e. 10 in hex is 16 in decimal. Notice that as the second hex symbol signifies lots of 16 you can write a large number with only two hexadecimal places. For example, FF is 255. As the next hexadecimal place is in terms of lots of 16x16, i.e. 256, with three hexadecimal symbols you can get as large as FFF, i.e. 4095.

Compactness is one of the advantages of hex. However, it is really useful because it is very easy to convert from hex to binary and vice versa. As a single hex symbol represents 0 to 15 and four bits also represents 0 to 15, you can convert a binary number to hex four bits at a time. For example:

```
0101 1110  = 5E
```

because 0101 is 5 and 1110 is E and both represent 94 in decimal.

Hex is really convenient for expressing the content of variables because two hex symbols specify a byte. So to specify the value of a `char` you only need two hex symbols, to specify an `int` you only need four or eight depending on whether it is a 16-bit or 32-bit number.

As already mentioned, C has hex literals signified by starting with `0x` and this is an almost universal convention for denoting hex even when not writing C. It is important to get used to reading hex and being able to convert between hex and binary.

If you are wondering why hex is preferred to octal notation, it is simply that a single octal symbol corresponds to just three bits. You need three octal symbols to specify a byte. Even so you will occasionally find octal used to specify a bit pattern.

Unsigned Integer Arithmetic

So far we have only considered representing positive integers, i.e. unsigned types. All unsigned integer types are a fixed number of bits in size and this raises the question of what happens when you add one to the largest value that can be represented. For example, an `unsigned char` with eight bits can represent 0 to 255 or 0x00 to 0xFF. What happens if you try to work out 255+1?

If you know the standard answer, you may never have considered the alternatives. For example, you could define 255+1 to be 255 - that is, once you reach the maximum value you don't go any higher. This is called saturation or clamped arithmetic and while most general purpose processors don't use it, some special devices such as DSPs (Digital Signal Processors) do.

What most general processors actually do is to roll over. That is, when you add 1 to 255 the answer is 256 which in binary is:

```
1 0000 0000
```

i.e. a 9-bit number. As this is being stored in an 8-bit variable then the natural thing to do is just ignore the ninth bit and let the answer be:

```
0000 0000
```

That is, $255+1=0$. This is rollover in the sense that a mechanical counter will roll over to the start when it goes beyond its maximum. It is as natural for a digital counter as for a mechanical one and it also turns out to be very useful, as we shall see.

Adding one to the largest representable value is often called overflow because the most significant bit of the result is lost. The term overflow suggests that it is an error but the C99 standard states that, for unsigned arithmetic, rollover is correct and not an error or undefined behavior.

Negative Numbers

Notice that as things stand we only have positive integers. Clearly this isn't going to be enough, we need to represent negative values as well. In non-computer arithmetic we simply write a minus sign in front of a value to indicate that it is negative. We can do the same with binary by treating the most significant bit as a "sign bit", i.e. 0 for a positive number and 1 for a negative number. This is simple to think up, but difficult to make work. Now when you are adding two numbers together, you have to look at the sign bits and work out if you should add or subtract. Even so, sign magnitude as it is called, is still in use. For example, 0011 is 3 in 4-bit sign magnitude and 1011 is -3.

There is a much better way of representing negative values which makes use of the standard integer arithmetic hardware found in nearly all processors. Consider for a moment the problem of finding what -x is. It is a quantity that when added to x gives you zero, i.e. $x + -x = 0$.

If you think back to unsigned arithmetic, you know that because of rollover you can get zero when you add a positive value to another positive value. For example, for an 8-bit char, we have 255+1=0. There is a sense in which 255 plays the role of -1. Similarly, in 254+2=0, 254 plays the role of -2 and so on. In general (256-x) plays the role of -x because (256-x)+x=256, which is zero in eight bits, i.e. 0x0000.

This representation of negative values is called two's-complement and if the number of bits in use is n then -x is given by 2^n-x. You can also see that this divides the total unsigned range into two ranges that represent the positive and the negative numbers. You can easily see this by starting to count at 0 and listing the corresponding two's-complement representation of the negative. For example, in eight bits we have:

```
+ 0 1    2    3    …  126 127
- 0 255 254 253 … 130 129 128
```

When you add the number in the first row to the number below it in the second row then the answer, allowing for rollover, is zero. Notice that when we reach 128 this behaves like -128 but there is no number that behaves like +128. That is, the ranges are 0 to 127 and 0 to -128.

In general, in two's-complement an n-bit value can represent -2^{n-1} to 2^{n-1}-1.

Two's-complement allows you to regard the most significant bit as a sign bit, even though we didn't set out to design things this way. However, you can no longer treat the other bits as the magnitude of the number.

When you do two's-complement arithmetic the same hardware is used as for unsigned ints. The only difference is the interpretation of what the bits mean. For example, in 8-bit char:

```
0xFD + 0x02 = 0xFF
```

and as unsigned this is:

```
253 + 2 = 255
```

but viewed as two's-complement it is:

```
-3 + 2 = -1
```

It is how you interpret the bits that matters, not what you do with them.

As well as two's-complement there is also one's-complement, which isn't used as much because it makes implementing arithmetic slightly harder. It is similar to two's-complement, but instead of subtracting from 2^n you use 2^n-1. One's-complement almost works with standard arithmetic but you have to add an "end around carry" rule. That is, any final carry from the most significant bit has to be added to the least significant bit. For this reason two's-complement is more or less the standard choice as it needs no additional rules.

The importance of one's-complement is that it makes it easy to get a two's-complement value. The one's-complement of any given value is simply the bitwise Not ~ of the binary representation. That is, the one's-complement of x is ~x, see Chapter 12 for bitwise operations. As the one's-complement is one less than the two's-complement, you can compute the two's-complement by adding one, i.e. -x =~x+1.

Two's-Complement Overflow

So in most machines negative numbers are represented as two's-complement values. Also notice that rollover is essential for two's-complement arithmetic to work, i.e. to give the right answer. However, it is possible for two's-complement values to overflow in a way that is different from unsigned ints. For example, suppose the value in a `signed char` is 127, the largest positive number that can be represented in 8-bit two's-complement, and you add one to it. The result is 128 which is -128 in two's-complement and you have created a negative number by adding two positive numbers.

Two's-complement arithmetic overflows when addition involving two positive numbers gives a negative result or two negative numbers give a positive result. Notice that you cannot get an overflow if one of the numbers is positive and the other negative.

The C library `limits.h` contains a set of constants that you can use to find what the largest value is for any type:

```
#include <limits.h>
```

For example, `UINT_MAX` is the largest value you can store in an `unsigned int` and `INT_MAX` is the largest value you can store in a `signed int`.

The most important thing to know at this stage is that signed overflow is undefined behavior and this means that in a well-formed program it can never occur. The reason that it is undefined is that the standards do not specify the representation for negative numbers, therefore what happens on overflow depends on the representation. In fact, it would be better if the standard just stated that what happened on overflow was what was natural for the representation in use.

The fact that signed overflow is undefined behavior is taken advantage of by optimizing compilers in ways that you might find surprising. In practice this only happens if you select an aggressive optimization option – but it does happen. For example, you can test for overflow after the fact using something like:

```
int x=INT_MAX;
if(x+1<x){
    printf("Overflow");
}
```

If you are using GCC with the `-02` option you will discover that you don't see the Overflow message! The reason is that the compiler has assumed that signed overflow does not occur because the program does not engage in undefined behavior and so it has removed the if statement as its body can never be executed.

The problem is that many C programs assume that signed arithmetic will always wrap with behavior given by two's-complement arithmetic. Without a way of turning off this undefined behavior, most of the C programs ever written would fail to compile or give the wrong result.

Most compilers will let you control how signed arithmetic is treated. For example GCC supports two options:

`-fwrapv`

which enforces wrapping at all times and:

`-ftrapv`

which generates a SIGABRT (SIGnal AboRT) which terminates the program.

If you compile the previous example using the `-fwrapv` option you will find that you do see the overflow warning and the result is what you would expect from a rollover.

The whole question of testing for overflow is a surprisingly difficult one for something you might have thought was solved a long time ago. In particular, for signed overflow you can't simply let the overflow happen and then test for it – that would be undefined behavior.

For example, you cannot simply use:

```
int result=a+b;
if(a>0 && b>0 && result<0)printf("Overflow \n");
if(a<0 && b<0 && result>0)printf("Overflow \n");
```

because if the overflow message is printed then signed overflow has occurred and this is undefined behavior.

You can avoid this with a slight rearrangement of the test:

```
if (a > 0 && b > 0 && a>INT_MAX-b)printf("Overflow \n");
if (a < 0 && b < 0 && a<INT_MIN-b)printf("Overflow \n");
```

You can see that the final term in the test is a way of testing for `a+b>INT_MAX` or `a+b<INT_MIN` without actually having to work out `a+b`.

You can make this slightly more efficient by dropping the initial test on `a`:

```
if (b > 0 && a>INT_MAX-b)printf("Overflow \n");
if (b < 0 && a<INT_MIN-b)printf("Overflow \n");
```

The reason is that in the first case `a>INT_MAX-b` can only be true if `a>0` and in the second `a<INT_MIN-b` if `a<0`.

In many cases you can be secure that overflow will not occur because of the values involved. You can also select a data type that is large enough not to overflow.

One good rule is to always used unsigned variables unless you really need negative numbers.

The problems of overflow are discussed in much more detail in ***Applying C For The IoT With Linux***.

Representations and printf

We have been using the print formatted function, `printf`, from the very start of programming in C – it is difficult to avoid. So far what it does hasn't been explained in any detail. The `printf` function converts bit patterns into human readable form.

The `printf` function takes a format string, strings are discussed in detail in Chapter 9, and a list of comma separated variables, and converts them into a formatted string of characters before displaying them on the standard output device:

`printf("format string", comma-separated list of variables);`

The way that `printf` works is that the *format string* is scanned and transferred to the result until a % is found. This signifies the start of a format specifier which controls the way the first variable in the comma-separated list will be formatted. Format specifiers come in a lot of forms, but the most basic are:

%d	integer
%f	float
%c	character
%s	string

So for example the most basic `printf` is just:

`printf("Hello World");`

in this case the format string has no format specifier and it is just copied to the output.

Slightly more advanced is:

`printf("The count is %d",count);`

This copies the format string to the output "The count is" until it hits the %d when it looks at the list of variables, takes the first one, and converts it from binary to a string representation of the integer. This isn't trivial. Consider the int variable storing the bit pattern 0..00001101, which is converted to the characters '1' followed by '3' i.e. the bit pattern is 13 in decimal. You can think of `printf` as converting a bit pattern into what a human thinks it represents. Notice that this conversion is completely determined by the format specifier you use. For example, %x will convert the bit pattern into hexadecimal symbols. In this case 0..00001101 is converted to the character 'D' i.e. 13 in hex.

You can take any sort of variable and ask for its bit pattern to be converted to characters in any way that you like. For example, if you initialize a char variable to be the character A you can printf it using %c when you will see the character A, or %d when you will see decimal 65, the character code for A.

```
char myChar='A';
printf("%c",myChar);
printf("%d",myChar);
```

No error messages are shown by the compiler, but you will see a warning from NetBeans suggesting the %c is more appropriate for a char. The point is that what the bit pattern represents is up to you. Other languages are more restrictive and insist that if you use a variable that is a character type then you should always treat it as a character. This is called strong typing and C is not strongly typed, although each new standard seems to try to make it more strongly typed.

If there are multiple format specifiers they are used to format the variable list one variable at a time.

For example:

```
printf("Count= %d efficiency= %f",count,eff);
```

will print the integer value in count in place of %d and the floating-point value in eff in place of %f.

Integer formatting is easy, but with floating-point numbers it is a bit more complicated as you can have different numbers of digits after the decimal point – in other words the human readable form is more variable. The full floating format specifier is %0n.mf, which specifies at least n characters wide and m decimal digits. So %4.2f means at least four characters wide and two digits after the decimal point, i.e., 0.12. The 0 following the % specifies that you want leading zeros included.

The same sort of idea applies to all of the format specifiers which take the general form, %w.pt, where w is the width, i.e. the minimum number of characters, p is the precision and t is the type of the conversion. The p specifier only has meaning for floating-point values. If you specify a width for a format then the value is padded with spaces, unless you include a 0 after the % when zeros are used. Padding is used to right-adjust the value, unless you add a – (minus) after the % when it is left-justified.

For example:

```
printf("%10s","abcd");
```

pads abcd to ten characters by adding spaces on the left whereas:

```
printf("%-10s","abcd");
```

pads to ten characters by adding spaces on the right.

Similarly:

```
printf("%10d",1234);
```

pads to ten characters using spaces on the left and:

```
printf("%-10d",1234);
```

adds the spaces on the right.

To pad with zeros on the left use:

```
printf("%010d",1234);
```

Padding with zeros on the right makes no sense.

You can also use the escape sequences – see Chapter 9 – for special characters.

For example:

```
printf("%10d \n",1234);
```

starts a newline after printing the value.

There are many other formatting details that you can make use of, but this is mostly all you need.

Summary

- Integer types can be regarded as storing a bit pattern with different possible interpretations. All bit patterns can be regarded as representing a positive integer.

- Hexadecimal is a good way of representing a bit pattern as it is short and easy to convert to and from binary.

- Unsigned integer arithmetic rolls over to zero when its range is exceeded. This is not undefined behavior.

- There are a number of ways of representing negative numbers, but two's-complement is the most common. It allows arithmetic to be performed as if the numbers were positive integers with the correct result when they are interpreted as two's-complement.

- Signed integer arithmetic overflows when its range is exceeded and this is undefined behavior.

- Testing for signed overflow has to be done before it happens and before undefined behavior has occurred.

- Printf will convert a bit pattern to a human readable form according to the representation selected by the format specifiers.

Chapter 6

Operators and Expression

One of the main workhorses of any computer language is the expression. This is often under-appreciated as we tend to think of the expression as simply a translation of arithmetic to a programming language – it is much more. The expression is a mini-language in its own right and consists of a set of rules for converting a set of individual data entities into a final result.

The most visible part of the set of rules is the operator which governs what is done to the data, but it isn't the only component of expression evaluation.

Evaluating Expressions

The main trouble with operators is that we know the four arithmetic operators so well that we tend to take them for granted and so miss most of the important ideas.

The best known example of an operator expression is the arithmetic expression, such as:

A=3+B*C

At first sight this looks like a single command to perform arithmetic, but it isn't. In fact it is a small program in its own right. It is composed of smaller commands and it has a flow of control.

This idea, that an expression is a small program, is remarkably obvious if you write in assembler because most assemblers don't support arithmetic expressions and so the expression program has to be written out using standard commands.

Notice that computers in general can't do arithmetic or any operation in a memory location. Instead the contents of the memory have to moved to a special internal memory location called a register. A register is a memory location that has additional hardware to allow operations such as arithmetic to be performed.

For example, using a single-register machine, the assembler equivalent of
A=3+B*C would be, using an easy-to-understand pseudo assembly language:

```
LOADREG   B   load the register from memory location B
MULTREG   C   multiply the register contents by C
ADDREG    3   add 3 to the register
STOREREG  A   store the contents of the register in A
```

This is much more clearly a little subroutine to work something out than
A=3+B*C is, but they are entirely equivalent.

Any compiler writer will tell you that the most difficult bit of any compiler is
the translation of expressions into good code. Well at any rate it used to be,
but now that the theory is reasonably well understood it's more or less a text
book exercise.

What makes operator expressions interesting is that they have a complex set
of rules for determining the flow of control through the component parts of
the expression.

For example, in the expression A=3+B*C all programmers know that the *
operation is done before the + operation but that doesn't correspond to the
order that they are written in.

In a simple left to right reading of the expression, the + should come first and
you do get different results depending on the order that the instructions are
obeyed. In a program the order of execution is usually from top to bottom
and/or from left to right so expressions really are different. The basic idea is
that each operator has a precedence associated with it and the order that each
operation is carried out depends on this precedence.

In the example above * has a higher precedence than + and so it is executed
first. Notice that this precedence can also be seen in the assembly language
version of the expression where the last part of the expression was evaluated
first.

Of course, you can always use parentheses to explicitly control the grouping
of the operators - an expression in parentheses will be treated as the single
value that it evaluates to - a sub-expression.

One subtle point is that although most languages, including C, evaluate
expressions according to precedence rules, most do not guarantee the order of
evaluation of sub-expressions. For example, in evaluating the expression:
(1+2)*(3+4)
the compiler can choose to work out (1+2) or (3+4) first. Of course, in this
case it makes no difference to the result, but there are exceptions -
specifically when the sub-expressions have side effects, i.e. change the state
of the program. There is much more to say about side effects later.

So far this is about as much as most programmers know about expressions,
but there is a little more. For example, an operator can operate on different
numbers of data values. The common arithmetic operations are dyadic or

binary, that is they operate on two values as in 1+2 but there are also plenty of monadic or unary operators that operate on a single value such as -2,

In general an operator can be n-adic without any difficulty apart from how to write them as part of expressions. For example, if I invent the triadic operator @ which finds the largest of three values, the only reasonable way to write this is as:

@ value1, value2, value3

and in this guise it looks more like a function than an operator.   This is because there is a very close association between functions and operators. Put simply, you can say that an operator is simply a function that has a priority associated with it. For example, rather than the usual arithmetic operators we could easily get by with the functions ADD(a,b), SUB(a,b), MULT(a,b) and DIV(a,b) as long as they had the same priorities assigned to them.

The question of how to write operator expressions neatly has exercised the minds of many a mathematician. The usual notation that suits dyadic operators, i.e. A+B is called infix notation, but it doesn't generalize to n-adic operators.

Operators in C

C has a range of operators that needs 16 levels of precedence to control! This bewildering array of operators is one of the reasons why C is intimating to the beginner and can look cryptic if written using lots of operators. You can always use parentheses to make the order of evaluation clear. A sub-expression in parentheses is always fully evaluated before it is used in the full expression.

Once you start to extend the range of operators that a language has then you have to worry about associativity as well as precedence. Associativity is simply the order that operators of the same priority will be evaluated. If you restrict your attention to simple arithmetic operators then the associativity isn't a problem because (A+B)+C is the same as A+(B+C). However, when you move on to consider more general operators it does matter. For example, in C the right shift operator A>>B shifts A right by B bits. (A>>B)>>C, which means shift A right by B+C isn't the same as A>>(B>>C), which shifts A right by the result of the right shift of B by C bits.

To make the result of such operations unambiguous, C defines each operator as associating left to right or right to left, i.e. right or left associative. The >> operator associates left to right because this means that A>>B>>C is (A>>B)>>C and this is the same as A>>(B+C).

Every operator in C has a priority and an associativity and you need to know both to be able to figure out what an expression evaluates to. You can see all of the standard C operators in the table on the next page.

Precedence	Operator	Description	Associativity
	++	Postfix increment a++	
	- -	Postfix decrement a--	
1	( )	Function call a()	Left-to-right
	[ ]	Array subscripting a[b]	
	.	Element selection by reference a.b	
	->	Element selection through pointer a->b	
	++	Prefix increment ++a	
	- -	Prefix decrement --a	
	+	Unary plus +a	
	-	Unary minus -a	
2	!	Logical NOT !a	Right-to-left
	~	Bitwise NOT ~a	
	(type)	Type cast (int) a	
	*	Indirection (dereference) *a	
	&	Address-of &a	
	sizeof	Size-of sizeof a	
	*	Multiplication a*b	
3	/	Division a/b	Left-to-right
	%	Modulo (remainder) a%b	
4	+	Addition a+b	Left-to-right
	-	Subtraction a-b	
5	<<	Bitwise left shift a<<b	Left-to-right
	>>	Bitwise right shift a>>b	
	<	Less than a<b	
6	<=	Less than or equal to a<=b	Left-to-right
	>	Greater than a>b	
	>=	Greater than or equal to a>=b	
7	==	Equal to a==b	Left-to-right
	!=	Not equal to a!=b	
8	&	Bitwise AND a&b	Left-to-right
9	^	Bitwise XOR (exclusive or) a^b	Left-to-right
10	|	Bitwise OR (inclusive or) a|b	Left-to-right
11	&&	Logical AND a&&b	Left-to-right
12	||	Logical OR a||b	Left-to-right
13	?:	Ternary conditional (see?: later)	Right-to-left
	=	Direct assignment a=b	
	+=	Assignment by sum a+=b	
	-=	Assignment by difference a-=b	
	*=	Assignment by product a*=b	
	/=	Assignment by quotient a/=b	
14	%=	Assignment by remainder a%=b	Right-to-left
	<<=	Assignment by bitwise left shift a<<=b	
	>>=	Assignment by bitwise right shift a>>=b	
	&=	Assignment by bitwise AND a&=b	
	^=	Assignment by bitwise XOR a^=b	
	|=	Assignment by bitwise OR	
15	,	Comma	Left-to-right

Notice that in C, ^ is exclusive or, not raise to a power as it is in other languages. Most of the other operators you either already know or they are discussed later. There are, however, some additional things to say about operators, in particular, casts and side effects.

Expressions, Type and Casting

There is a great deal of misunderstanding about type and casting in particular. In C it is better to think of a memory location as somewhere that happens to be currently in use to store a bit pattern that has a particular interpretation. For example, as explained in Chapter 5, the bit pattern 01000001 could be the binary representation of 65 or it could be the ASCII code for 'A' or it could signify that switches 0 and 6 are closed and the rest are open. The bit pattern stays the same, the interpretation changes.

In C, unlike in other languages, the type assigned to a variable or pointer only changes how the bit pattern is supposed to be interpreted and determines the amount of memory allocated. For example:

```
char myChar;
```

allocates a single byte which is interpreted, mostly by the programmer, as a character. So you can initialize it to a character literal:

```
myChar='A';
```

which stores the bit pattern 01000001 in the byte.

So is myChar a character or a number? If you are expecting a firm answer to this question you haven't yet understood the very loose way that C treats type. The best answer is that there is a bit pattern stored in myChar and it's up to you to how to interpret it. The compiler does expect you to treat it as a character and it will warn you if you treat it as something else, but it's just helpful advice to avoid you making a mistake.

Suppose that you really know what you are doing and you want to use char as if it was a numeric value and want it to be clear that you are doing this on purpose? The answer is that you can use a cast, which in C is denoted as a type enclosed in parentheses – (type). A cast is often optional as the compiler can work out what is going on, but it still useful to indicate to a human what you intend. Compilers will also often warn you that you are treating one type as a different type, but this is a helpful feature of the compiler and not something that is built into the C language.

A cast is written in front of a variable to tell the compiler that you want its bit pattern to be reinterpreted as the new type. Notice that this is a very simple process in most cases. Other languages often do a lot more work when you cast from one type to another.

For example, if myVar is an int then you can cast it to unsigned int using

```
(unsigned int)myVar;
```

However, what you get when you cast depends on the representation in use. For example:

```
int myVar1 = -1;
unsigned int myVar2 = (unsigned int) myVar1;
printf("%d \n", myVar1);
printf("%u \n", myVar2);
```

Here myVar1 is a signed int and set to -1 in two's-complement, but when it is assigned to myVar2 its bit pattern is interpreted as 4294967295. If one's-complement were in use then the bit pattern, and hence the final positive value, would have been different.

You can also change the size of a variable with a cast. If you cast from a smaller variable to a larger – a widening cast – then extra bytes are added. For example:

```
int myInt=(int) myChar;
```

Here myChar is just a single byte and, assuming int is four bytes, three bytes have to be added.

You might at this point think that the extra bytes should be zeroed and this is what happens for unsigned casts. If you start out with a negative int and cast it to a wider type then adding zero bytes would change its sign. To stop this happening, signed types use sign bit extension to set the additional bytes. For a signed type if the most significant bit is a zero then the extra bytes are zeroed. If the most significant bit is a one then the extra bytes are set to one. This preserves the value in the narrower type within the wider type. For example:

```
signed char myChar=1;
int myVar1 = (int) myChar;
```

In this case, the bit pattern in myChar is 00000001 and this is transferred to the low-order byte of myVar1, the remaining bytes are all set to 0 and both myChar and myVar represent 1 in two's complement. However for:

```
signed char myChar=-1;
int myVar1 = (int) myChar;
```

In this case, the bit pattern in myChar is 11111111 and this is transferred to the low-order byte of myVar1, the remaining bytes are all set to 1. In this case both myChar and myVar represent -1 in two's-complement.

In C the intent of a cast is to leave the bit pattern unchanged and simply interpret it in a different way. There is one small complication in that the C99 standard says that when you assign from a signed value to a unsigned value, what happens if the value cannot be represented (i.e. it was originally negative) is implementation-dependent. What this means in practice is that the bit pattern is simply interpreted as a positive number – the implementation-dependent part is simply taken to be the representation used for the negative range.

An assignment to a narrower type also follows the same pattern of trying to preserve the value of the bit pattern, but this time it might not be possible. What happens is that the wider type is truncated to the smaller size. If the value still represents the original value then so much to the good, if it doesn't then you don't get any warnings or error messages.

Put simply, if the wider type is storing a value that is representable by the narrower type, then copying just the lower bytes transfers the value unchanged for signed and unsigned values. Notice that when the value in the wider type cannot be represented by the narrower type what you get depends on the representation used by the machine for negative values. For example:

```
char myChar;
int myVar=1024;
myChar= (char) myVar;
printf("%d \n",myChar)
```

In this case myVar stores 1024, which cannot be represented in a single byte, and so the assignment works, but does not preserve the value. The lower byte, which is zero, is transferred to myChar and so we see 0 printed.

Now consider:

```
char myChar;
int myVar=-1024;
myChar= (char) myVar;
printf("%d \n",myChar);
```

This too prints 0 because the value stored in myVar cannot be represented in a single byte and the lower byte in myVar is zero, but if one's-complement was used for negative values, the result would be 1. What you get depends on the representation in use.

The rule is:

◆ if the types in the cast are the same size then the bit pattern is unchanged and just reinterpreted as the new type.

◆ Casting a signed type to an unsigned type is implementation dependent.

◆ In a widening cast the extra bytes are zeroed for unsigned types or the sign is extended for signed types

◆ In a narrowing cast the lower bytes are used for the new bit pattern.

The exception to the rule "don't change the bit pattern" is a cast to a floating-point type. In this case the value is preserved at the expense of the bit pattern. For example:

```
int myInt=3;
myFloat=(float) myInt;
```

results in myFloat containing 3.0 and the relationship between the bit patterns in the two variable is complicated. In casting from a floating point type the same technique is used and any fractional part is lost. For example:

```
int myInt;
float myFloat=3.1415;
myInt=(int) myFloat;
```

results in myInt containing 3. You don't need the explicit casts because the rule is that the results are automatically cast to the type of the variable being assigned to.

One of the important uses of casts is in the evaluation of expressions with mixed types. When you write an expression that involves different types the compiler attempts to find casts that make all of the types the same. It first performs integer promotion. Notice that this occurs even if all of the types are involved are chars. That is, chars are cast to ints and this clearly doesn't change any values. For example:

```
unsigned char myChar=255;
int myInt;
myInt= myChar*255;
printf("%d",myInt);
```

In this case the result 65025 is printed because, although the arithmetic should overflow, both the values are converted to int before the calculation is performed. The expression is evaluated as if it was:

```
myInt= (int) myChar* (int) 255;
```

If there are types "larger" then int then casts are implicitly performed to promote everything to the largest size involved in the expression. The order is:

```
int < long<  long long < float < double < long double
```

and the unsigned types have the same rank as the corresponding signed type.

The rules, known as the usual arithmetic conversions seem complicated. The C99 standard says:

1. *If both operands have the same type, then no further conversion is needed.*

2. *Otherwise, if both operands have signed integer types or both have unsigned integer types, the operand with the type of lesser integer conversion rank is converted to the type of the operand with greater rank.*

3. *Otherwise, if the operand that has unsigned integer type has rank greater or equal to the rank of the type of the other operand, then the operand with signed integer type is converted to the type of the operand with unsigned integer type.*

4. *Otherwise, if the type of the operand with signed integer type can represent all of the values of the type of the operand with unsigned integer type, then the operand with unsigned integer type is converted to the type of the operand with signed integer type.*

5. *Otherwise, both operands are converted to the unsigned integer type corresponding to the type of the operand with signed integer type.*

The most worrying part of this specification is point 3 as converting a signed integer to an unsigned of the same rank seems to invalidate the arithmetic. You have to remember that two's-complement arithmetic works even if you consider the value to be unsigned. For example:

```
unsigned int myUnsigned=1;
int myInt=-1;
myInt=myInt+myUnsigned;
printf("%d \n",myInt);
```

In this case the signed int is converted to unsigned and it looks as though we are going to get the answer 2 as the negative is lost. This is not how it works. The signed int is converted to an unsigned int with the same bit pattern. When added together the roll over occurs and the result is the same in two's-complement. That is, it prints 0 and we have the correct answer.

This doesn't mean that you cannot get the wrong answer. For example:

```
unsigned int myUnsigned=UINT_MAX;
int myInt=1;
myInt=myInt+myUnsigned;
printf("%d \n",myInt);
```

In this case you will still see zero printed, which in this case is probably the wrong answer. Again we have the same bit patterns. The UINT_MAX is -1 when regarded as a signed int and hence the final result is zero. To get the correct answer we need to explicitly use a cast to long long:

```
unsigned int myUnsigned=UINT_MAX;
int myInt=1;
long long mylong= (long long)myInt+(long long)myUnsigned;
printf("%lld \n",mylong);
```

In fact, we don't need to cast myInt to long long because the rules will promote it to the same as myUnsigned.

Notice that these casts are only performed in expressions, including comparison operators, and bitwise operators. They are not performed for assignment operators. In most cases the result of expressions involving mixed types give you the correct answer but if in doubt use explicit casts.

A common idiom, however, is to rely on the rules to change integer arithmetic into floating-point arithmetic. For example:

```
int myInt=1;
float ans=myInt/100;
```

gives the answer 0 as integer division is performed before the result is converted to a float. However:

```
int myInt=1;
float ans=myInt/100.0;
```

gives the result 0.01 as the literal is now a float and hence myInt is automatically converted to a float.

Side Effects

An important idea in C is that assignment is treated as a dyadic operator with the lowest precedence. The operator = stores the value on the right-hand side in the variable on the left-hand side and then its result is the value of the right-hand side. Put more academically you can say that the result of A=B is B but the operator has a side effect of storing the value of B in A.

In general side effects are bad ideas because they spoil the purity of the picture of an operation that combines a number of values to give a result. For example, in A=B+C the + has a higher priority so B+C is evaluated and then the result is used in A=result.

Treating assignment as an operator means that you can, if you really want to, write expressions like D=(A=B)+C, which first evaluates A=B to give B and as a side effect stores this in A and then adds C to B and assigns this to D.

Notice that == is the test for equality in C and so A==(B=C) assigns C to B and tests if C is equal to A in a single expression. The brackets are necessary because == has a higher priority than =.

Taking this a little further, C also allows other operators to be combined with the assignment operator. For example, A+=1 translates to A=A+1. In this case += operator has the value A+1 which it stores in A as a side effect.

Another subtle point concerns what A*=2+3 evaluates to? Is it (A*2)+3 or is it A*(2+3)? The answer is that it is A*(2+3) even though the * should have a higher priority than the +. The reason is of course that the *= operator has a lower priority than * or + i.e. it is a new operator not a combination of two operators.

Postfix and Prefix Increment

Once you have introduced the idea of a side effect as part of the assignment operator you might as well carry on and introduce other operators with side effects. For example, the unitary operator ++ when used as a postfix operator in A++ returns current value of A. That is, it is the same as just writing A, but as a side effect it increments A. In other words, if A is 3 then after B=A++, B is set to 3 and A is set to 4. Notice that this is quite different from ++A, the corresponding unary prefix operator, the result of which is A+1 and which has the side effect of incrementing A. So, if A is 3 then, after B=++A, B is set to 4 and so is A. Notice that the ++ postfix operator has the highest priority and associates from left to right, whereas as a prefix operator it has a priority of 2 and associates from right to left. Also notice that A++ has the same meaning as A+=1.

It is this amazing richness of operators that makes C so attractive to anyone who has taken the time to master it. After a while you can write an expression such as:

```
C += A++ + B++ + (D=++E) == F
```

I have to admit that it would take me time to work out exactly what this expression does and then I would quickly forget it! The best advice is, don't write expressions that are an effort to understand. Just because you have access to a dangerous weapon it doesn't mean you have to use it.

Conditional and Comma

Finally, there are two operators that deserve special attention. The first is the conditional operator. This is a functional alternative to an if statement. It allows you to includes a conditional within an expression. The expression:

```
expression1?expression2:expression3
```

first evaluates expression1 and treats it as a Boolean. If this is true, i.e. non-zero, then the result is expression2, but if it is false, i.e. zero, then the result is expression3.

For example:

```
int ans= a<0?-1:1;
```

sets ans to -1 if a is negative and 1 otherwise.

The advantage of the conditional expression is that it is an expression and can be used as part of a larger expression. For example:

```
int ans =(a<0?-1:1)*size;
```

sets ans to -1*size or 1*size depending on the value in a.

The comma operator, as distinct from other uses of the comma, is perhaps the most puzzling in C. The comma is only treated as an operator if it is part of an expression:

```
expression1, expression2;
```

First `expression1` is evaluated and the result is thrown away. Then `expression2` is evaluated and it is returned as the result.

For example:

```
int ans= 1+2, 3+4;
```

this evaluates 1+2 and ignores the result and then evaluates 3+4 and stores this in `ans`.

The big problem with the comma is not what it does but working out what you need it for.

The obvious answer is that you want it when an expression has a side effect that you are interested in more than its result.

For example:

```
int ans= i++,a+i;
```

first increments `i` and then stores a+i in `ans`.

You still might not be convinced of its usefulness and in this you would be right. One of its more common uses is to allow for multiple expressions within the parts of a `for` loop.

For example:

```
for(i=1,j=9;j>0;i++,j--){
    printf("%d %d ", i, j);
}
```

Notice that we initialize both `i` and `j` and that `i` increments and `j` decrements each time through the loop. The result is a loop in which `i` runs from 1 to 9 and `j` from 9 to 1. There are alternative clearer ways of writing this loop. If you find you are using the comma operator a lot, you probably need to think about how other programmers are going to understand your programs.

Sequence Points and Lazy Evaluation

We have introduced the idea of a side effect in a casual way. In principle, an expression should simply evaluate to a result and no changes should occur to any variables or the state of the program or machine. Such an expression is said to be "pure". C has a number of "impure" operators which create side effects and the fact that you can use a function within an expression means that side effects are very likely. A function, as discussed in the next chapter, can do almost anything and change the state of the system in ways that are not at all apparent or even connected with the expressions they are used in.

When you first meet the idea of side effects they can seem simple and useful, but what does:

```
i=i++;
```

mean?

It all depends on when the increment is performed relative to the assignment. The problem is that the value of i is changed twice by the side effects of the expression and it isn't clear what order the side effects occur in.

For many years this problem was ignored and it was left to the compiler writers to provide a definition in each case. However, for C11 an attempt was made to solve the problem but its approach isn't really as helpful as it might be. It makes use of the idea of a sequence point – a point in the evaluation of a function when all side effects of operators so far encountered are guaranteed to be complete – and the C11 standard defines several of them.

The end of any full expression obviously has to be a sequence point – i.e. assignment, return expression, if statement, switch, while, do.. while and each expression in a for loop. The end of an initializer is also a sequence point and so is the comma operator and any function call in an expression. In addition side effects are complete before the function is called. Notice, however, that the order in which the functions are called is not always specified and the order in which parameters are evaluated is not specified.

There is a sequence point after the evaluation of each format specifier in a printf to make sure that any expressions you are evaluating don't interact in undefined ways.

When it comes to the internal details of expression evaluation it makes sense to define some operators as sequence points.

Logical OR || and AND && operators are sequence points because they are evaluated in a different way to other operators. For an OR, if the left-hand expression is true then the right-hand expression is not evaluated because the result is already known to be true. Similarly for an AND, if the left-hand expression is false then the right-hand expression is not evaluated because the result is already known to be false. This is called short circuit, or lazy, evaluation. In both cases, however, the left-hand expression is complete, including side effects, before the right-hand expression is evaluated. Notice that if the right-hand expression has any side effects, including throwing an error, these will not happen if the evaluation is short circuited.

For example:

```
int result =a||b++;
```

b will not be incremented if a is true and in:

```
in result = a|| b/0;
```

no divide by zero error will occur if a is true.

For similar reasons, a conditional expression is a sequence point. The first expression is fully evaluated including side effects before the second or third expression is evaluated. That is the ? in a?b:c is a sequence point.

So far sequence points simply tell you when you can expect side effects to be complete, but they don't help with the problem of:

```
i=i++;
```

The sequence point is at the end of the expression and it still isn't clear whether the side effects occurred as assignment then increment, or increment then assignment. To deal with this the C11 standard also introduced two conditions that have to be satisfied to make an expression legal:

> *Between the previous and next sequence point an object shall have its stored value modified at most once by the evaluation of an expression. Furthermore, the prior value shall be accessed only to determine the value to be stored.*

These two rules make i=i++ undefined as the variable has its value changed more than once. The second condition also makes expressions such as:

```
array[i]=i++;
```

undefined as, even though i is only modified once, its original value is used to determine where the result is stored and not just what the result is.

Many programmers find the C sequence rules difficult to understand and apply, but this really isn't the problem. If your code causes you to contemplate the role of a sequence point or the conditions that apply then you are probably writing expressions that should not be written.

It really shouldn't need a rule to convince you that writing:

```
i=i++;
```

is a bad idea. In general, relying on side effects isn't a good idea unless their role and meaning is very simple and very clear. If an expression has you wondering exactly what it means then it will make you or some other programmer wonder what it means the next time you see it, even if you manage to work out its meaning this time around.

Summary

- Expressions form a sophisticated programming language in their own right consisting of operators with precedence and associativity rules.

- Casts allow bit patterns to represent different things.

- Widening casts always preserve the original value.

- Narrowing casts only preserve the original value if it is representable in the smaller type.

- The rules for mixed type expressions are complicated - if in doubt use an explicit cast.

- Sequence points determine when the side effects of an expression are determined and sequence point rules make some expressions undefined.

- Logical OR and AND are lazy evaluated which means that the right-hand expression may never be evaluated and hence may never cause any side effects.

- If you find you are having to work out sequence points and rules the chances are you are writing obscure code.

Chapter 7

Functions, Scope and Lifetime

You can't get far in creating C programs without using functions. The good news is that in C, functions are simple and efficient and there is no reason not to use them. In this chapter we look at functions, parameters, pass-by-value, return values, prototypes, local and global variables.

C is a very small language in the sense that it has very few pre-defined keywords. Many of the things that you use in C are provided by libraries of functions. For example, as we discovered in a previous chapter, C doesn't have a print command and instead makes use of the `printf` function provided by the stdio library. As we will now learn, functions can be added and existing functions modified and this makes C a more powerful language.

First we need to discover what a function is exactly and how to create one.

What is a Function

A function is just a collection of C instructions that you can execute by simply using the function's name. For example, `printf` is a function and it is comprised of quite a few lines of C statements. You can call up those lines of C by simply typing `printf`. In this sense you have already been using functions since your first C program.

A function is a block of C code that you give a name.

We already know how to create a block of C code - you simply write it between curly brackets as a compound statement. A function assigns a name to this block of code using the syntax:

```
functionName(){block of code}
```

For example, if you start a new C99/C11 project and before main enter:

```
hello(){
 printf("Hello Function World");
}
```

This defines a function called "hello" which simply prints to the console the message Hello Function World.

You can use the function by typing its name followed by parentheses:
`hello();`

You can think of this as transferring control to the start of the function which then executes each instruction to the last instruction when the part of the program that called the function is resumed.

The entire program is:

```
hello(){
 printf("Hello Function World");
}
int main(int argc, char** argv) {
 hello();
 return (EXIT_SUCCESS);
}
```

If you run this you will see the message displayed in the console.

Notice that you have to place the hello function before the main program because functions have to be defined before they are used, just like variables. As we will shortly discover, you can also declare a function before its use or definition.

Why Functions?

You can see that functions are a powerful idea. In the first example you have effectively added a new command to C - the hello command.

This idea of extending the language by writing functions is a basic approach to creating larger programs. In top-down programming you write functions that do big things by calling other functions that do smaller things by calling other functions that do even smaller things - until the program is complete.

In bottom-up programming you write small functions that might be useful and then use them to build functions that do bigger things by using them and so on up to the final program.

Most programmers think that top-down is the right way to go because it is easier to see what you need at each level. You can write your top-level functions first just assuming that the lower-level functions that you need can be created later. This is called stepwise refinement and it is one of the most powerful methods of creating programs.

Of course, you don't need functions at all. Instead you can write your program as a single block of basic C instructions. However, trying to work out what this monolithic bock of code does when you come back to it after even a few hours can be very difficult. Splitting a program up into small functions makes it much easier to understand and this is called modular programming. Your program shouldn't be one huge chunk of code - it should be made of modules each one doing a clear and understandable job. In C functions are your modules.

The only possible argument against using functions is the efficiency objection. Using a function is slower than just writing the instructions because the flow of control has to transfer to the function and then back again to the program that called the function. True, there is an overhead in calling a function, but it is small enough to be ignored in most situations. Of course, there are times when developing programs on small devices that you need every drop of performance. Even in this situation it is still worth using functions unless you are forced not to.

Thinking in functions should be your default that you only give up when efficiency really forces you to. Even then, the performance gain in removing functions for the equivalent code is usually negligible.

Parameters

You might have been wondering what the parentheses are for in the definition of a function? The answer is that you can include parameters that the calling code can use to tell the function what to do.

For example:

```
hello(int times) {
  for (int i = 0; i < times; i++) {
    printf("Hello Function World \n");
  }
}
```

You can see the intent here. The function has an integer parameter `times`, which is used in the for loop to repeat the message that number of times. The \n at the end is the symbol for a newline and this separates our messages onto separate lines – more about this in Chapter 9.

To use the function in its new form you would write:

```
hello(3);
```

to display the message three times.

What happens is as if a new variable had been created and set to 3 within the function, i.e. as if:

```
int times=3;
```

was the first instruction in the function.

The variables you use when you define a function are usually referred to as parameters and the values you supply to define the parameters when the function is called are usually referred to as arguments. So in our example, `times` is a parameter and 3 is an argument.

This is a completely general mechanism and you can pass in multiple parameters to a function, each one separated by a comma.

For example:

```
add(int a, int b) {
  int c = a + b;
  printf("%d", c);
}
```

This adds the two specified parameters together and prints the result. You call the function using:

```
add(1,2);
```

which displays 3 on the console.

Return Values

Parameters are ways of getting values into functions. There is also a way of getting a result out of a function - its return value. If you write:

```
return value;
```

in a function it terminates and the value specified is returned.

What does "returned" mean?

The returned value is the value of the function when it is evaluated and this can be used in an expression or assigned to a variable.

So for example, if you change the add function to:

```
add(int a, int b) {
  int c = a + b;
  return c;
}
```

then it now returns the sum of a and b, i.e. the value stored in variable c.

You can now use add and the value it returns:

```
int ans = add(1, 2);
printf("%d",ans);
```

which prints the value 3.

It is as if add was a variable that had its value determined by the return value of the function.

Notice that while you can send multiple inputs into a function, i.e. use multiple parameters, there can only be a single return value. This can cause problems, but it is easy enough to overcome this limitation, as explained in Chapter 11 on structs.

There is a small complication. Notice that we have to specify the type of the parameters, but the return type isn't specified at all. In fact if you don't specify a return type then the compiler (in C99) assumes that the value is an int. In general, you should always specify the type of the return value by prefixing the function name with a type.

So the add function should be more properly defined as:

```
int add(int a, int b) {
 int c = a + b;
 return c;
}
```

Now we have a function that accepts two ints and returns an int and it is used exactly as it was before. The advantage of typing the parameters and the return value is that the compiler can check that you are working with the right type of data and flag an error if you try to do something silly.

As long as a function returns a value of the correct type it can be used within an expression as if it was a variable of that type. For example:

```
int ans=add(1,2)*2;
```

will store 6 in ans.

void

What if a function doesn't return a value? This is allowed. Sometimes a function just does something and doesn't need to return a value. For example, the hello program, our first example of a function, simply prints a value and returns without a return value. You can include a return statement anywhere within a function to bring it to an end, with or without a return value.

For example:

```
hello(){
 printf("Hello Function World");
 return;
}
```

It is good practice to always include a return statement within a function.

One final complication. How do you indicate the type of a function that doesn't return a value?

The answer is to use the type void. This makes C programs look mysterious but all it means is something like "nothing" or "not applicable".

So the hello program really should be written:

```
void hello(){
 printf("Hello Function World");
 return;
}
```

You will discover that C tends to use the term "void" when anything isn't of a fixed or known type.

The main Function

If you look again at any C program you will now recognize the main program as more correctly the main function - `main` is just a standard function that is automatically called when your program is loaded. It then proceeds to get the work done by calling other functions.

```
int main(int argc, char** argv) {
  lines of code that call other functions
  return (EXIT_SUCCESS);
}
```

The only thing that might puzzle you at this stage are the strange looking parameters. To understand these in detail we will have to find out about pointers in a later chapter.

Declaring Functions

So far we have followed the rule that a function is declared before we attempt to use it. This results in all the functions used in a program being listed first and then the code that uses them. To many programmers this is the wrong way round. They want to read the main program first and find out what it does and then read the functions that it uses and then the functions that they use and so on. This mirrors the procedures and philosophy of stepwise refinement, where the top level functions are defined first and the functions that these call are created later. If it makes sense to create a program in this order, it also makes sense to read it in this order.

You can place a function's code anywhere within the file, or even in another file as long as you include a short declaration - a prototype - for the function before it is used. A prototype simply specifies what the types are that are used in the function declaration.

For example, the add function's prototype is:

```
int add(int,int);
```

which declares that the add function takes two int parameters and returns an int. You can include parameter names if you want to, but the general practice is to strip the prototype down to just the types.

As long as the prototype is included in the file before the first use of the function, everything will work. The full declaration of the function can be later in the file or in another file altogether. The prototype provides enough information for the compiler to check that you are using the function correctly. Later it will become clear that the best place for function declarations is a `header.h` file. This provides everything you need to make use of the function, but not its implementation which can be found elsewhere.

There is one subtle point to look out for. A function with no parameters is declared as:

```
void myfunc(void);
```

If you declare it as:

```
void myfunc();
```

this is taken to mean any number of parameters. You might think that there is no difference between the two, but only the use of void will allow the compiler to notice if you declare a function as having no parameters and then go on to provide a definition that does have parameters.

The Expression Principle - Pass-by-Value

There is a general principle in C that anywhere you can use a number you can use an expression that evaluates to the same type of value. Until now we have been setting parameters to values, but in fact you can pass a function an expression and this will be evaluated before the function is executed.

For example:

```
hello(3*2);
```

in this case the multiplication is performed and 6 is passed to the function.

Of course an expression can involve variables.

For example:

```
hello(3*count);
```

in this case the value in count is multiplied by 3 and the result passed to the function.

The limiting case of an expression is just a variable:

```
hello(count);
```

In this case the value in count is passed into the function.

This is usually called pass-by-value and it is one of the possible ways of passing data into functions. It is one of the simplest and you should now be able to understand what happens in the following example:

```
void test(int a){
  a=1;
}
var a=0;
test(a);
```

The question is what does a store after the function call?

Is it 1, which is what it was assigned in the function, or is it its original value of 0?

The answer is that it still holds 0.

There is no connection between variables outside of the function and the parameters inside the function even if they have the same names. Because of the use of pass-by-value what happens is that the value of a is passed to the function's parameter which also happens to be called a. When you assign to a in the function it is to a completely different variable than the a outside of the function.

This gives rise to the rule that modifying variables inside a function has no effect on variables outside of the function. This is good, because it makes functions into isolated little chunks of code that are easy to understand and check.

There are parameter passing methods that do allow functions to change things outside of their own code and these are more dangerous, even if they are sometimes useful. C only uses pass-by-value and we will have to see how to achieve other ways of passing parameters later. It is also important to know that sometimes pass-by-value can look like pass-by-reference and this is the case when we come to work with arrays and strings in the next chapters.

Inline Functions

Functions are the best way to organize your program – a function for every identifiable task. Some programmers worry that having so many functions is inefficient. The overhead is the time taken to call the function and the time for the return. In practice this overhead is usually well worth the improvement in program maintainability. However, sometimes a function does so little that it it seems that it might be better to code it each time it is needed. Inline functions give you the best of both worlds, but they were only introduced in C99.

Any function that is marked as inline has its call expanded as if its body had been written in place of the call. However, things aren't quite as simple as this. The inline qualifier is only a hint to the compiler to inline the function. If the compiler decides not to then you will get an error from the linker as there is no non-inline version of the function defined. To avoid this you can mark a function as static.

For example:
```
static inline int add(int a, int b){
    return a+b;
}
int main(int argc, char** argv) {
    int c= add(2,3);
    printf("%d \n", c);
    return (EXIT_SUCCESS);
}
```
It is usually said that you don't need to use inline with modern compilers as they will optimize your code without the help of your suggestions.

Local Variables – Lifetime and Scope

This idea of functions being isolated chunks of code goes beyond just the parameters. You can declare variables within a function and these are generally called local variables, also known as auto variables.

For example, in the add function we declared a local variable c:

```
int add(int a, int b) {
 int c = a + b;
 return c;
}
```

Just like the parameters this c has nothing to do with any variables called c outside of the function. The local variable c is created when the function starts executing and it is destroyed when the function returns. That is, local variables only exist while the function is running - they have the same lifetime as the function. This also means that local variables can only be accessed from with the function they are defined in – that is, they have local scope.

This should all seem very reasonable to you but if you forget it you will try to write something like:

```
int counter(){
 int c=0;
 c=c+1;
 return c;
}
```

and in main:

```
printf("%d \n", counter());
printf("%d \n", counter());
```

The idea here is that c is incremented by 1 each time the function is executed but of course this doesn't work. The variable c is destroyed each time the function returns and so it doesn't matter how many times you call counter(), c is created anew and set to 0 and then has one added to it. The function always returns 1.

If you want a variable to exist for longer than the function is executing then you have to declare it to be static. A static variable is allocated in an area of memory that is not destroyed when the function comes to an end.

For example, the attempt at a function counter can be rewritten as:

```
int counter(){
 static int c=0;
 c=c+1;
 return c;
}
```

With this change it works. Notice that you can initialize a static variable and this is only performed once when the variable is created.

It is important to realize that a static variable declared within a function is still local to that function. In other words, `static` extends the lifetime of a variable, but not its scope. A local variable is by default `auto`, but as this is the default you rarely see the qualifier used. That is:

```
auto int c;
```

is the same as:

```
int c;
```

Notice that, unlike other languages, C does not allow you to define functions inside other functions. That is, in C there are no local nested functions. This is generally not a big problem, however, as there is block scope.

Block Scope

Mostly variables that are local to a function are all that you really need to create a program, but C (from C86) actually supports block scoping. You already know that you can use curly brackets to create a "compound" statement or block. What is less well known is that any variables that you declare within a block are scoped to that block. That is, any variables you declare in a block are local to that block and override or hide any variables declared earlier in a containing block by the same name.

For example, if you write in a main function:

```
int a = 1;
printf("%d \n", a);
{
    int a = 2;
    printf("%d \n", a);
}
printf("%d \n", a);
```

you will see 1,2,1 printed. The first declaration of a is local to main. The second declaration is local to the block and overrides the variable defined in the function. When the block ends the block scoped variable is destroyed and the original is in scope.

The most common use of block scope is in a for loop, an extension introduced in C99, when you write:

```
for(int i=0;i<10;i++){}
```

In this case the variable you declare within the for loop is block scoped to the block that follows. That is, it overrides any similar variable in the containing block and it is destroyed on leaving the block. This means you can reuse the variable name without having to worry about changing any variable already declared. However, it does mean that you cannot access the final value of the loop.

For example:

```
int i=42;
for (int i = 0; i < 10; i++) {
    printf("%d \n", i);
}
printf("%d \n", i);
```

prints 0 to 9 and then 42.

The same rules apply to variables declared within while, while..do and if statements, although use of this is far less common.

You can nest blocks within other blocks and the inner block can access the variables of any containing block as well as its own block scoped variables:

```
int a = 1;
printf("%d \n", a);
{
    int a = 2;
    printf("%d \n", a);
    {
        int b = 42;
        printf("%d %d n", a, b);
    }
}
printf("%d \n", a);
```

In this case you will see 1,2,2,42,1 printed. The inner block can see the a declared in the first containing block.

You can see that in this sense a function is just an example of a block scope, although you cannot, in standard C, define a function within a function. You can define as many blocks within a function as you want. There are also a number of different extensions, GCC for example, that allow nested functions, but the best advice if you want to write portable code is to ignore them.

Opinion is also split on the usefulness of block scoping. It is very useful when used in for loops to isolate the index from the rest of the program. It can also be used in the same way to divide up the "namespaces" within a program or function to reduce accidental interactions. However, if you can identify a block of code that benefits from this isolation then you have probably identified a block of code that should be a function in its own right.

The general advice is to use functions to structure your program, not blocks.

Global Variables – Program and File Scope

If there are local variables, are there global variables?

The answer is yes.

In C global variables are often called "file-level" variables because they are declared outside of any function. A global variable will automatically be zeroed to a value that is appropriate for its type, but it is usually better to initialize it. The most important thing about global variables is that they are created when the program starts and remain in existence until the program ends. They can also be accessed from within any function. The only exception to this is if the function declares a variable of the same name. Then the local variable is used, overriding the global variable.

As a global variable exists for the lifetime of the program, you can use it to keep track of things throughout the execution of the program. So now the counter function can be made to work:

```
int c=0;
int counter(){
 c=c+1;
 return c;
}
```

Now if you put:

```
printf("%d \n", counter());
printf("%d \n", counter());
```

in main, you will see 1 followed by 2 and the variable c is being used to count the number of times the function has been used.

By comparison with static variables introduced in the previous section you could say that a global variable is a static variable with global or program scope.

If you declare a program scope variable in one file, how does the compiler know, when you use it in another file, that it is defined elsewhere? The answer is that a program scope variable is declared in one file but re-declared using the extern qualifier in any other file that has code that wants to use it.

So in fileA.c you might write:

```
int myGlobal=42;
```

and in fileB.c you would write:

```
extern int myGlobal;
```

Notice that you don't initialize a program scope variable in files that make use of it. There is much more to say about extern in Chapter 14.

You can also specify a global variable to be static but this doesn't modify the lifetime of the global variable – it makes it slightly less global. A global variable is in scope in any compilation unit in a project i.e. it has program scope. A static global variable is only in scope in the current compilation unit – it is said to have file scope. A compilation unit is what you get when you take a single.c file and expand it by adding all of the includes – see Chapter 14.

When you first start to construct larger programs there is a tendency to create lots of global variables because this means you don't have to pass them as parameters to functions. The functions can just make use of global variables as if they were their own. The problem is that global variables are not the property of any function and they have to be hard-coded into the functions.

Using lots of global variables produces a program that is fragile in the sense that any small change can have effects further away from where the change occurred. Using functions and local variables makes programs up out of small isolated units that can be understood and debugged in isolation.

Scope Summary

C supports three levels of scope:

- **block scope** – applies to variables that are declared within a block or function. They are accessible only within the block and within nested blocks, and they live only as long as the block is being executed. The auto qualifier is optional and rarely used.

- **file scope** – applies to variables that are declared outside of any function or block and with the static qualifier. Such variables live for the entire life of the program but they are only accessible in the file that they are declared in.

- **program scope** – applies to variables that are declared outside of any function or block and without the static qualifier. Such variables live for the entire life of the program and are accessible in any file that includes a declaration of the variable with the `extern` qualifier.

You will also hear of a fourth scope – function scope – but this applies only to labels and not variables. Any label you define is usable anywhere in the function it is defined in.

Heap and Stack

So far we have looked at how functions are declared and used, and how local and global variables behave. You really don't need to know much more than this, but it all makes a lot more sense when you understand the memory model that lies behind this behavior.

When you declare a new variable the compiler has to generate code that allocates sufficient memory to store the data it is to hold. The whole subject of memory allocation is a complicated and interesting one, but every programmer should know about the two very general approaches - the stack and the heap.

Stack-based memory is a natural match for the way that variables are allocated and created by a program constructed as a set of nested function calls - which most are.

What happens is that, when a function is called, all of its local variables are created on the top of the stack, creating its so called stack frame. While the function executes it only has access to its local variables. That is, its entire environment is limited to the data on the stack frame. Exceptions to this local-only rule are global variables and dynamic storage, see Chapter 10, and these are allocated on the heap. You can think of the heap as an area of memory that can be accessed by any function.

If the function calls another function then the new function creates its stack frame on the top of the stack. In this way each new active function can allocate its own local variables in its own portion of the memory owned by the stack. The beauty of stack allocation is that all that has to happen to implement garbage disposal is that, when each function returns, it simply clears the stack of its stack frame. It does this by adjusting the stack pointer to point to the end of its stack frame, so returning the memory to use. Of course, when a function ends, control returns to the method that called it and it finds the stack in just the state it needs to access its own local variables.

In this way each function gets access to its local variables while it is running without any need to keep track of where they are. The stack is also used to store parameters and return values passed between methods in a fairly obvious way. It also is the mechanism that implements block scope.

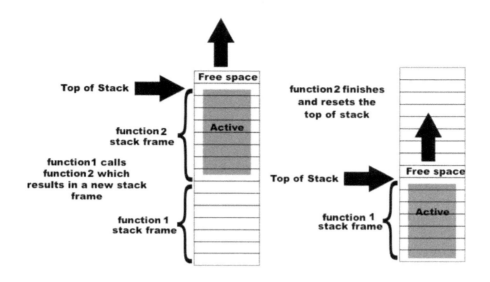

The stack in action

The stack works well for storing all manner of data that is created and destroyed following the pattern of function calls, but for global data, and for very large or complex data, we need something else.

The alternative is the "heap". This is a very descriptive name for an area of memory that is set aside simply for the purpose of storing global data. When a global object is created, an area of the heap is allocated, which is big enough to store it at its initial size. A reference to its location is returned - often to be stored in a local variable on the stack. However, unlike local variables which are created and destroyed along with the function they belong to, there is no clear signal that a global object is finished with. It doesn't necessarily become redundant when the local variable that it was initially created with goes out of scope because there could be many variables referencing it.

In other languages there is automatic heap garbage collection. Memory that is no longer used is automatically deallocated and returned to the heap. In C there is no garbage collector. In the case of global variables the memory is allocated until the program ends. In the case of dynamically allocated memory you have to explicitly free the memory you have allocated. That is, the responsibly for acquiring and releasing heap memory is down to the programmer. If you allocate memory and then forget to free it once you have finished using it, you have created a memory leak. This is much worse if the program repeatedly allocates new heap memory and then fails to release it. In such a case the memory used by the program steadily increases until the system cannot allocate any more memory and the process is killed.

Even though C doesn't have automatic garbage collection, Linux does have a heap manager, but its task is to make sure that each process has its own heap and that blocks of heap memory are available on demand. In practice, there are a number of different heap managers using different algorithms. In most cases you can ignore the details of heap management and simply rely on memory being looked after.

Notice that it is generally better to adopt a throwaway approach to heap use. For example, if an object, a string say, needs to increase in size then, rather than try to open up some space to make the current allocation bigger, it is generally better to allocate a whole new block of memory. Although this involves copying the existing object to the new location it is often efficient and safer, as long as you remember to free the memory used by the old string.

Storage on the stack fits in with the idea of local variables and the call and return pattern of functions. Storage on the heap gives rise to data objects that are better regarded as global, but with possible local references to them.

Summary

- A function is a block of code that can be executed by using its name and can have a set of parameters and a return value.

- You have to specify the data type of each parameter and the return value. If there is no return value then use void to indicate its type.

- The main function is simply a function that the system starts running when your program is loaded.

- Functions have to be defined before they are first used unless you include a prototype which gives the return type and parameter types before the first use.

- If you specify a prototype for a function that has no parameters you should use void as in int myfunction(void). Using empty parentheses means that the number of parameters is unknown.

- Parameters are passed by value to the function and any changes to the parameters do not affect any variables in the calling program. This makes functions isolated chunks of code.

- Variables declared inside functions are local variables. They only exist while the function is executing and they have nothing to do with any variables of the same name anywhere else in the program. This makes functions isolated chunks of code. Local variables are also known as auto variables.

- More generally, auto variables have block scope. Blocks can be nested and an inner block can see all of the variables of a containing block.

- Variables that are declared static as apposed to the default auto have the same lifetime as global variables but they have block scope.

- Global or program variables are declared outside of any function. They live for the entire life of the program and can be accessed by any function without needing to be passed as parameters. The extern qualifier has to be used to allow code in other files to use the variable.

- A global variable declared as static has it scope restricted to the current file – file scope.

- If a function defines a local variable of the same name then this takes precedence - it overrides the global variable of the same name.

- The different types of variable reflect the underlying memory technology. Auto variable are stored on the stack and this is why they have block scope and lifetimes. Global/static variables and dynamic data are stored on the heap and have global lifetimes.

Chapter 8

Arrays

The most useful data structures in almost any language are arrays and strings, and they are particularly important in C. As you might expect, the implementation of both is closer to the hardware than in most other languages.

In this chapter we take a look at how arrays are used and how pointers play a role. This is a first look at pointers as it is important that you know they exist and what they are, but there is a full chapter later on which explains the more advanced aspects of pointers. In the next chapter we look at the practicalities of using strings.

The Array

The array solves many problems that would be next to impossible without it. Suppose you need to keep track of the scores of three users. You might well try:

```
user1=42;
user2=43;
user3=44;
```

This works, but now generalize it to 100 users or a 1000. Not easy, but with an array it's very easy. An array is a data structure that consists of lots of repeats of a basic element. Any element can be accessed using a numeric index.

So, for example, the previous user scores using an array would be written:

```
user[1]=42;
user[2]=43;
user[3]=44;
```

Notice that the array is called user and it has three elements.

In C you have to declare an array and fix its size before you can use it using an instruction like:

```
type name[number of elements];
```

So for example to declare an array of three `ints` you would use:

```
int user[3];
```

The only potentially confusing part is that the array index starts at zero. This means that the declaration creates `user[0]`, `user[1]` and `user[2]`. Notice that the declaration gives the number of elements not the value of the final index.

It is important to realize that an array cannot increase or decrease in size once it has been declared.

There are also some confusing rules about how you can specify the size of an array. For arrays defined at file level, i.e. not within a function, the size must be specified as a constant expression. A constant expression is one that can be evaluated at compile time as all of the values are known, e.g. `2*3`.

For an array defined within a function, you can use an expression that can only be evaluated at runtime, but only in C99 or later – this is known as a variable length array or VLA. In C89 the GCC compiler will allow runtime expressions and only warn you that you shouldn't do this if you add `-pedantic` to the compiler options. What this means is that you can include arrays in functions and set the size when the function is used.

For example:

```
int sum(int n){
    int myArray[n];
    . . .
}
```

is fine in C99 and later and works in GCC's implementation of C89 even if it isn't part of the standard. Notice that as n isn't defined at compile time you cannot say what the size of the array is before the program is run. When the function is completed the array is destroyed as is the case for any local variables. If the function is called again then the array is recreated possibly with a different size. In most cases VLAs are best avoided if at all possible.

It doesn't matter how you specify the size of an array, once declared it cannot change its size without being destroyed and recreated.

You can also initialize an array using curly brackets:

```
int myArray[6]={0,1,2,3,4,5};
```

This sets `myArray[0]` to zero, `myArray[1]` to one and so on. If you don't provide enough initializer values then the remaining elements are set to zero. This can be used to set an entire array to zero.

For example:

```
int myArray[1000]={0};
```

notice that this only works for zero.

C99 also allows you to specify starting positions for the initialization.

For example:

```
int myArray[1000]={0,1,2, [10]=10,11,12,13,[500]=500,501};
```

This sets the first three elements to 0,1 and 2, then zeros elements up to 9 and stores 10 in element 10, 11 in 11 and so on, then zeros 14 up to element 500 where it stores 500, and 501 in element 501. You can see the idea, the initialization restarts at the indicated position in square brackets and any elements not initialized are set to zero.

If you don't specify the size of the array then it is made large enough to hold all of the initial values:

```
int myArray[]={0,1,2,3,4,5};
```

Also notice that while ints have been used in the examples, all of this works no matter what the types of the elements are.

For example:

```
float myArray[]={1.0f,2.0f,3.0f};
```

creates a three element array of floats.

Arrays and For Loops

So now you know how to create an array and how to initialize one. However, how would you initialize an array with 1000 elements?

The answer, as it is to many uses of the array, is to use a for loop. Arrays and for loops were made for each other. For example, to set a 1000-element array to 1 you would use:

```
int myArray[1000];
for(int i=0;i<1000;i++){
    myArray[i]=1;
}
```

The array index isn't restricted to be a simple variable, it can be an expression. You can also assign an expression to an array element. It is this freedom to use expressions that makes C a powerful language. In general anywhere you can use a variable or a literal you can use an expression.

For example, to set the array elements equal to 0, 2, 4, and so on you would use:

```
int myArray[1000];
for(int i=0;i<1000;i++){
    myArray[i]=2*i;
}
```

One of the things you have to learn to use C effectively is how to construct index expressions that give you the array elements you want to use. For example, assuming i runs from 0 to the last element:

```
2*i
```

gives you all the even elements and:

```
2*i+1
```

gives you all the odd elements.

For example, to set all the even elements to 1 and the odd elements to -1 you would use:

```
int myArray[1000];
for(int i=0;i<500;i++){
    myArray[2*i]=1;
    myArray[2*i+1]=-1;
}
```

Once you have seen this sort of approach then you can usually work out an expression that gives you what you need.

Assigning Arrays - Pointers

When you have two variables, x and y say, then when you assign x to y:

```
y=x;
```

the value in x is copied to y and after this any changes that you make to y don't affect x.

This is value assignment and it is what you generally expect to happen.

Now consider assigning variables that are storing arrays:

```
int x[10]={0,1,2,3,4,5,6,7,8,9};
int y=x;
```

If you try this out you will see a warning message and the program won't do what you expect. The reason is that y has been declared as an int and what is assigned to it is an int array.

The way that arrays are implemented is different to the way simple values like ints are implemented. When you create an array, what is stored in the variable is not the array, but a pointer to the start of the array, i.e. to the first element of the array. Arrays are stored somewhere in memory and the variable is just a pointer to the data. Exactly how this all works is described later. What is important for the moment is to understand that the variable stores a pointer to the data.

You can think of a pointer as the address of the start of the array. In most cases this is accurate but machines have a range of different addressing mechanisms that can sometimes make the relationship between a pointer and a low-level machine address more complex. However, in the case of the x86 and ARM architecture you are relatively safe in thinking of a pointer as an address.

The type of an int array is signified by `int*` which means "a pointer to int", more of this in Chapter 10. You can create a pointer to any simple data type by following the type by an asterisk. For example, `float *` is a pointer to a float and so on.

Now if you try:

```
int x[10]={0,1,2,3,4,5,6,7,8,9};
int* y=x;
```

it all works, but it still might not be doing what you expect. It doesn't copy the array in x into y, i.e. this is not a value assignment, and no new copy of the array data is created. Instead, of course, x doesn't store the array data, but a pointer to the array data. The assignment is still a value assignment, in the sense that what is stored in x is copied to y, but what is stored in x is a pointer to the start of the array data.

Now both x and y point to the same block of data and any changes made using variables x or y change the same block of data.

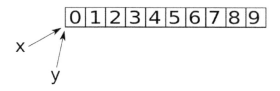

For example:

```
x[0]=1;
y[0]=2;
```

both change the first element of the same data. As y is used last, the final value of the first element of the array is now 2. That is, variables that reference arrays are pointers to the start of the array and this results in reference semantics.

Notice, however, that when you assigned x to y the value in x was copied to y, value semantics applied, but in this case the values were pointers.

When you assign an array variable to another variable it is the reference that is copied and both variables point to the start of the same data.

This idea of a pointer is very important in C and Chapter 10 explains it in all its details, but it is important that at this early stage you have an idea of how pointers and arrays work.

So what do you do if you want a new copy of an array that you can work on without changing the original?

The answer is the for loop yet again:

```
int x[10]={0,1,2,3,4,5,6,7,8,9};
int y[10];
for(int i=0;i<10;i++){
    y[i]=x[i];
}
```

Notice that you have to declare y as y[10] to allocate the storage for the copy of the array.

If you get the size of y wrong then it is possible that your program will write data into areas of memory that haven't been allocated to it. This is an array overrun or overflow.

For example:

```
int x[10]={0,1,2,3,4,5,6,7,8,9};
int y[5];
for(int i=0;i<10;i++){
    y[i]=x[i];
}
```

As y is only five elements long, where is x copied to after the fifth iteration? The answer is whatever area of memory comes after the allocated five elements of y. The GCC compiler will warn you that at iteration five you have undefined behavior, but it will still compile and run the program for you.

This is another example of how C is a low-level language that can get you into trouble if you do things incorrectly.

Multi-Dimensional Arrays

Some languages have an additional construct to create arrays with more than one dimension. C simply uses the same mechanism it uses for a one-dimensional array to create arrays with two or more dimensions.

For example, a 2D array is simply an array of arrays:

```
int myArray[10][10];
```

This defines an array of ten elements each of which is in its turn an array of ten elements. So for example:

```
myArray[0];
```

is the first element of the array of ten elements and so it is an array with ten elements. This means that:

```
myArray[0][0];
```

is the first element of this array of ten elements and hence it is an int.

You can see how myArray can also be thought of as a 2D array, table or matrix with a typical element:

```
myArray[i][j];
```

being the element in the ith row and jth column – if you think of the array as being made of rows and columns.

You can initialize a 2D array in the usual way:

```
int myArray[2][2]={{1,2},{3,4}};
```

which again corresponds to the idea of an array of arrays.

Just as a single for loop goes naturally with a one-dimensional array, a pair of loops, one for the rows and one for the columns, goes naturally with a two-dimensional array:

```
for(int i=0; i<n; i++){
    for(int j=0,j<m; j++){
        myArray[i][j]=0;
    }
}
```

In this case i indexes the n rows and j indexes the m columns.

As in the case of one-dimensional arrays, there is a range of expressions involving the indices that can be used to access and store values in the array.

For example:

```
for(int i=0;i<n;i++){
  myArray[i][i]=1;
}
```

sets just the diagonal elements to one.

Another common idiom is:

```
for(int i=0; i<n;i++{
  for(int j=0; j<i; j++) {
    myArray[i][j]=0;
  }
}
```

zeros just the lower triangle of elements.

Arrays as Parameters

We have looked at how simple types are passed in and out of functions, but now we have to look at a slightly more complicated case – passing arrays to functions and returning arrays.

The first thing to know is that you have to indicate that what you are trying to pass into a function is an array. You don't have to specify the size of the array, just that it is an array. To do this use a pair of empty square brackets. For example, a function that sums all of the elements in an int array to get a total is fairly easy:

```
int sum(int myArray[],int n){
    int total=0;
    for(int i=0;i<n;i++){
        total=total+myArray[i];
    }
    return total;
}
```

Notice that the myArray parameter has to have [] following it to indicate that it is an array rather than an int. Also notice that we have to pass the size of the array as a final parameter.

If you want to declare the function then you can use a function prototype:

```
int sum(int myArray[], int n);
```

or, using the rule that you don't have to specify the parameter names in a function prototype:

```
int sum(int[], int);
```

As before, you can think of int[] as being the type of the parameter, i.e. an int array, but you can only use this notation in a function prototype.

You can call this function in the way you would expect:

```
int myArray[1000]={1,2,3};
int total=sum(myArray,1000);
printf("%d",total);
```

This all seems reasonable, but there is something new. If you change the value stored in an element then you change the value in the original array.

That is, it appears that arrays are passed by reference and not by value.

For example, a function that zeros an array is possible:

```
void zero(int myArray[], int n) {
    for (int i = 0; i < n; i++) {
        myArray[i] = 0;
    }
}
```

This will zero any array that you pass it and notice that it isn't necessary to return the array as a result. The changes made in the function affect the array in the main program.

In fact this is still pass by value, but what is being passed is the value of a pointer to the start of the array. The gives the function the address of the start of the array and this is used to work directly with the original array, so making it look as if the array has been passed by reference. There is much more to say about pointers in Chapter 10.

Arrays and Return

What about returning an array result?

At first this looks very simple and a lot like passing an array into a function, but there is a significant problem that it is important to be aware of as early as possible.

First, you can return an array as the result of a function, but as functions can change arrays that are passed in, you generally don't have to.

For example, adding a return to the zeroing function doesn't actually help:

```
int* zero(int myArray[], int n) {
    for (int i = 0; i < n; i++) {
        myArray[i] = 0;
    }
    return myArray;
}
```

Once again we are using int* to mean an array of int elements. You can't use int[] to indicate the type of the return of a function. Now myArray is returned as the result of the function. If you use the function with something like:

```
int* newArray=zero(oldArray);
```

where oldArray already exists in the program, then you don't get what you might think you get.

As with simple array assignment, no copy of the array is made by returning an array or assigning the result. The oldArray variable points to the array data and the function uses the passed in pointer to change the array data, i.e. to zero it. When the function returns myArray it returns a pointer to the same array data. So in the main program we now have two variables which reference the zeroed array data – the original oldArray and the newly created newArray. In the sense that both variables point to the same data, returning myArray hasn't achieved anything.

Returning an array that was passed into a function may be pointless, and it may be confusing, but it is relatively harmless. A much more dangerous misunderstanding is in most attempts to return an array from a function that wasn't passed into the function. For example, consider this, almost useful, modification to the zero function:

```
int* zero() {
    int myArray[10];
    for (int i = 0; i < 10; i++) {
        myArray[i] = 0;
    }
    return myArray;
}
```

The only difference is that now the function defines an array, zeros it and then returns it as its result.

What could possibly be wrong with:

```
int* newArray=zero();
```

Surely, newArray is now an array of ten elements all zeroed. In fact newArray points to an array of ten elements that no longer exists. As myArray is declared as a local variable within the function, it and anything it references no longer exists when the function terminates.

You cannot create and return an array, or any other C data structure, from a function because it is local to the function.

There are ways of doing the job, but the proper solution requires knowledge of the C memory model, dynamic memory allocation, and so on, and these are discussed in later chapters.

The quick fix is to declare the array as `static`. This ensures that the array exists after the function has completed and forces it to be non-local:

```
int* zero() {
    static int myArray[10];
    for (int i = 0; i < 10; i++) {
        myArray[i] = 0;
    }
    return myArray;
}
```

With this change the function works. However, it doesn't matter how many times you call the function, it will return the same `myArray`. That is, it doesn't manufacture a new array each time it is called, there is just the one instance – but at least it doesn't crash. To find out how to create a new array on each call of the function we need to look into memory management – see Chapter 10.

Returning pointers to data that has been created within a function and no longer exists is a common and difficult-to-debug problem and it is not just confined to arrays.

The Problem of Size

When C was first developed there was a choice to make. Do you record the size of data structures like arrays along with the array? The initial choice was to simply allocate the memory needed to store the data and not waste space by storing extra data to keep track of sizes. The job of keeping track of sizes was handed over to the programmer. What this means is that there is no way of finding out the size of a data structure like an array at runtime.

There is the `sizeof` operator which will return the size of any variable or data type in terms of how many char sized variables occupy the same space. That is, `sizeof(char)` is always 1 and a `char` typically, but not always, takes 1 byte. In the rest of this explanation it will be assumed that 1 `char` takes 1 byte for simplicity.

For example:

```
sizeof(int);
```

is 4 or 8 depending on the number of bytes used for an int on a particular system. Notice, however, that this is determined at compile time. The compiler looks up the number of bytes that an int takes and substitutes a constant of the correct value.

If you apply sizeof to a variable then it gives you the number of bytes it takes to store the variable. The only exception to this rule is if the variable is declared as an array. In this case the space needed for the variable isn't worked out but the space needed for the array is.

For example:

```
int myArray[1000];
printf("%d", sizeof(myArray));
```

prints 4000 on a typical machine with an sizeof(int) being 4 bytes. Notice that this is worked out at compile time – the compiler determines the size of the array and substitutes 4000 in place of sizeof. There is nothing dynamic going on here.

Notice that you can use this to work out the number of elements in the array. That is, the number of elements in an array is given by:

```
n=sizeof(myArray)/sizeof(myArray[0]);
```

the total size of the array divided by the size of a single element in bytes.

At this point you might think that you can use this to find the size of an array passed to a function – you can't.

For example:

```
int sum(int myArray[]) {
    int total = 0;
    for (int i = 0; i < sizeof(myArray)/sizeof(myArray[0]); i++) {
        total = total + myArray[i];
    }
    return total;
}
```

this returns a compiler warning that sizeof(myArray) will return the size of a pointer to myArray. The reason, which is discussed in context in Chapter 10, is that when you pass an array to a function, any trace of it being an array is lost. What is passed is a pointer and this is what sizeof reports on and returns usually 4 or 8. It is usually said that the array "decays to a pointer" when passed as a parameter to a function.

In C99 you can use sizeof to determine the size of a variable length array created in the function.

For example:

```
void zero(int n) {
    int myArray[n];
    for (int i = 0; i < sizeof(myArray)/sizeof(myArray[0]); i++) {
        myArray[i] = 0;
    }
}
```

This works in C99 but not in earlier versions and in this case you can see that sizeof is computed at runtime as n is not known at compile time. In most cases this isn't a useful facility because you generally know the size of the array from the expression used to declare it, i.e. n in this case.

As a result of all of this C cannot determine the size of an array passed to a function which is not determined at compile time. This is a problem because you often want to write a function which works on an array and guarantees not to go outside of the allocated memory.

There are three broad approaches to remedy this:

1) Pass the size of the array into the function as a separate parameter. This is what we have been doing in most of the examples so far.

2) Use a special marker for the end of the array – this is the approach strings use and this is explained in the next chapter.

3) Don't use an array but choose a more sophisticated data structure that records its size as another data entry. This is a good solution, but isn't as efficient as using raw arrays.

This all seems reasonable, but the real problem is that there are standard library functions which do not check for array size and are prone to buffer overflow. Today there are safe versions of all of these functions that require you to specify the size of the array as an additional parameter.

For example, the function gets will read characters from the keyboard until the user types newline and store the result into a char array. No attempt is made to specify the size of the char array to gets and hence if the user types too many character the array will overflow. However, the fgets function can be used for the same job and allow you to specify the size of the char array and it will stop reading in if the user enters more characters than the array can hold.

Using functions that protect you from overrun is a big part of making a program secure. This topic is explained in more detail in the next chapter.

Enumerations

One of the standard uses of an array is to store data relating to specific labels. For example, suppose you wanted to record the number of hours you worked in a week. You might want to write something like:

```
work[mon]=9;
```

C enumerations were designed to allow you to do exactly this and similar tasks. Notice first that the basic way to do this job would be to assign integers to days, Sunday=0 and so on. So:

```
work[mon]=9;
```

would be:

```
work[1]=9;
```

An enumeration is just an assignment of integers to labels.

For example:

```
enum week {
  sunday=0, monday=1, tuesday=2, wednesday=3,
          thursday=4,friday=5,saturday=6
}
```

This declares a new data type – enum week. In fact you don't need to list the values because if you leave them out the compiler assumes you mean values from 0 increasing by one to however many values you need. In other words you could have written the above as:

```
enum week {
  sunday, monday, tuesday, wednesday, thursday,friday,saturday
}
```

If you do use explicit assignment then you can assign any integer values you like, i.e. they don't have to be in order.

You can use this to create a variable that can only take on the values you have listed.

For example:

```
enum week work;
```

now you can write

```
work=monday;
```

Notice that monday is not a variable. The compiler looks up monday in your definition of the enum and replaces it by the integer you set it to. However work is a variable and it is just a plain old int.

In other words:

```
enum week work;
work=monday;
```

is converted to:

```
int work;
work=1;
```

which you can check with:

```
printf("%d",work);
```

which prints 1.

Notice that as monday isn't a variable and it isn't an lvalue you can't assign to it and:

```
monday=9;
```

generates an error.

To return the original example, recording work hours for each day of the week. This can be done by declaring an array of type enum week:

```
enum week work[7];
```

Now you can write:

```
work[monday]=9;
```

Notice that work is an array of int and the compiler converts the instruction into:

```
int work[7];
work[1]=9;
```

You can also write things like:

```
for(enum week day=sunday;day<=saturday;day++){
    printf("%d\n",work[day]);
}
```

But it is worth keeping in mind that the compiler converts this into:

```
for(int day=0;day<=6;day++){
    printf("%d\n",work[day]);
}
```

In other languages this sort of transformation would be called "syntactic sugar" to indicate that it wasn't a real addition to the language, just something that makes it more readable. This is about the only syntactic sugar C provides.

You can use enumerations in other contexts than arrays and for loops. One particularly common use is to implement `options` that can be combined using bitwise logical operators – see Chapter 12.

Another is to define what looks like a boolean type using:

```
enum bool {false,true};
```

After this you can declare a variable that appears to be a boolean. For example:

```
enum bool myBool;
myBool=true;
if(myBool) …
```

Notice that this `myBool` is still an `int` and `true` is 1 and `false` is 0.

In Chapter 11 we meet the `typedef` statement which can be used to define synonyms for types. Using this we can get rid of the need to use `enum` in all declarations. For example:

```
typedef enum {false,true} bool;
```

```
bool myBool=true;
if(myBool)…
```

Although this sort of approach is commonly used it can become confusing and lead to errors. If you can't work with C99 and `bool` it is better to explicitly use ints and 0 and 1 for false and true.

Summary

- The array is the most fundamental of the simple data structures and it is declared using type name[number of elements].

- In C all arrays start from zero e.g. myArray[0] is the first element.

- Array sizes in C are best regarded as fixed. C99 allows variable length arrays, but these are best avoided if at all possible.

- You can initialize arrays at compile time using a list of comma separated constants in parentheses.

- Arrays and for loops are a natural fit. The index in a for loop is often used to access particular array elements.

- Often you have to work out an arithmetic expression involving the index that will give you the array elements that you need.

- The variable that is created when you declare an array is a pointer to the first element of the array.

- When you assign one array variable to another, value assignment applies, but the value copied is a pointer, i.e. a reference to the first element of the array, and this results in reference semantics.

- Multi-dimensional arrays are created using the same array mechanism, but in this case creating arrays of arrays and so on.

- Arrays can be passed as arguments to functions, but what is passed is a pointer to the first element.

- You can return an array from a function, but in most cases this isn't necessary. Returning an array that has been created within the function is also not a good idea because the local variable that references it will be destroyed when the function exits.

- Finding the size of an array is a compile time operation in C before C99.

- Enumerations can make working with arrays seem easier, but they introduce no new features to C.

Chapter 9

Strings

This is going to be a shock if you program in almost any other language - C doesn't actually have strings in the sense of most languages. All it has are char arrays and a few conventions on how these are used. It is still important to know how these work and there are some extra features over and above a simple array.

Strings

In most other languages, strings are a special additional data structure managed by the runtime software. In C a string is just an array of chars.

For example:

```
char myString[10];
```

is an array of 10 chars or a string depending on how you look at it. As already mentioned a char is usually an eight bit byte, but it doesn't have to be.

As in the case of a general array, myString is a pointer to the first element of the array.

That's all there is to it and it is important you keep this in mind as you find out about the extra features that are generally associated with string use in C.

The problem with using strings in C is the same problem we have with finding the size of a more general array. Generally strings are processed character by character. So how do you know you have reached the end of a string?

You could record the length of every string you use and specify it in any functions you use or create. However, this is not what C encourages you to do. In C strings are "null-terminated". That is, the last character of every legal string is a null, i.e. a zero byte. You can say that a char array isn't a string unless its null-terminated and this is the difference between the two.

For example, in:
```
char myArray[3]={'a','b','c'};
char myString[4]={'a','b','c','\0'};
```
myArray is a standard char array and myString is a null-terminated char array i.e. a string. Notice that single quotes are used for character literals and \0 is the escape character for a null char. Notice also that myString is one element longer than myArray and this is the small overhead of using null-terminated strings.

The usual way of initializing a string is to use a string literal, which is signified using double quotes and supplies a null terminator by default:
```
char myString[4]="abc";
```
or, more usually, we leave out the explicit size of the array:
```
char myString[]="abc";
```
Notice that it is sometimes important to allocate more storage to a string than it actually uses so that you can lengthen it using string operations.

For example:
```
char myString[10]="abc";
```
is a null-terminated string with three chars followed by a null. The remaining six elements are available to extend the string should it later be required.

Notice that you can only use a string literal to initialize a string. Unlike other many other languages you cannot write:
```
myString="def";
```
myString is an array of chars and assigning to it in this way doesn't make any sense. To assign to a string you need to use the built-in strcpy function or similar – see later. String assignment involves copying the pointer to the start of the string and this applies to literal assignment as well.

You can use escape characters within the string literal:

\0	Null
\\	Literal backslash
\"	Double quote
\'	Single quote
\n	Newline (line feed)
\r	Carriage return
\b	Backspace
\t	Horizontal tab
\f	Form feed
\a	Alert (bell)
\v	Vertical tab
\nnn	Character with octal value nnn
\xhh	Character with hexadecimal value hh

This also brings us to the question of what the character encoding is?

As already explained in Chapter 4 the data type char is the smallest of the integer types. It is called char because traditionally it was used to store single byte ASCII codes representing characters. Today we have additional problems in that text is represented by Unicode, of which ASCII is only a tiny subset. Unicode is supported in C99 by the introduction of the wide character type but exactly how this was to be used wasn't specified. C11 introduced a completely new way of working with Unicode and again this has not proved to be popular.

Some operating system functions require the use of wide character types using UTF-16 encoding and in this case you have little choice but to look up the documentation and convert strings to UTF-16.

To work with Unicode strings the simplest thing to do is adopt UTF-8 encoding and put up with the fact that sometimes a character needs more than one byte to represent it. Most of the string functions will work with UTF-8 without modification, with the proviso that a character might correspond to more than one element of the string. For example if you use a function to find the length of the string you will get the number of bytes used but this may be more than the number of characters as some characters need two or three bytes to store. You can consider ASCII to be the characters that can be represented as a single byte in UTF-8.

Working with Unicode in general is a tricky subject and not a core concern for most IoT and systems programs which have limited user interfaces, and for the remainder of this book strings will be treated as ASCII or a UTF-8 subset.

String Handling Functions

C, the core language, has minimal string support but the standard library has extensive string functions. It is important to know that the majority of the standard functions, all those with names starting with str, work with null-terminated strings. If the string or strings that they accept are not null-terminated then you will almost certainly encounter an array overflow.

Before getting on to the string functions it is worth pointing out that as a C string is just a char array you can directly access any character by indexing. That is:

```
char myString[10]="abc";
myString[2]='X';
```

changes c to X.

You can also add to a string if there is enough space, but remember to fix up the null terminator:

```
char myString[10]="abc";
myString[3]='X';
myString[4]='\0';
```

To make use of the string functions you have to add:

```
#include <string.h>
```

One of the first functions to discover is the strlen function which returns the length of a string.

For example:

```
char myString[10]="abc";
printf("%d",strlen(myString));
```

displays 3 as the length of the string even though the length of the char array is 10. If you are used to other languages and know a little about how they work you might expect strlen to retrieve a value that gives the string length but as already explained C strings are null-terminated. What strlen does is to scan the string to find the first null, counting the non-nulls on the way.

You can write your own strlen function quite easily:

```
int myStrLen(char string[]){
    int i=0;
    while(string[i]!=0){
        i++;
    }
    return i;
}
```

This isn't the most compact way to write strlen but it does make it easy to understand.

What happens if you pass strlen a string that isn't null-terminated?

The same as happens for all str functions – the loop keeps going until it hits a memory location that contains a zero by chance. If you are lucky this will just give you an incorrect result. If you are less lucky then it will probably try to read some other program's data and cause a crash.

Other commonly used string functions are:

- ◆ strcat - concatenate two strings
- ◆ strchr - string scanning operation
- ◆ strcmp - compare two strings
- ◆ strcpy - copy a string

Using these is generally obvious.

Two examples should help.

To concatenate two strings you need to make sure that the first string has enough storage available to store both strings:

```
char myString1[10] = "abc";
char myString2[] = "def";
strcat(myString1, myString2);
```

You can see that myString1 has storage for 9 characters plus a null terminator and so it has space for the extra three letters. The three characters in myString2 are copied into myString1 starting at the null and myString2's own null finishes the string. Notice that there is a lot that can go wrong with this and no check is done to make sure that there is sufficient space and no checks that the strings are null-terminated.

The strchr function will find the position of a single character in a string:

```
char myString1[10] = "abc";
char* position=strchr(myString1,'c');
```

This sets position to point at the first occurrence of c in myString1 or a null pointer if c isn't in the string. Notice that this is not the array index of the element but a pointer to it. That is, position can be regarded as the substring of myString1 starting at the first occurrence of c including all the characters to the end and the null. Also notice that this is not a copy of the string. Again, if the string isn't null-terminated this will overrun the char array.

A very common use of string functions is to assign to a string. As mentioned earlier, you cannot use an idiom like:

```
char myString[10]="abc";
myString="def";
```

to assign to a string variable. You have to use the strcpy function:

```
char myString[10]="abc";
strcpy(myString,"def");
```

Notice that this only works if the destination has enough space to store the new string and its null terminator. If the source is a general string and not a string literal you also have the potential for an array overrun if it isn't null-terminated.

You can see the general pattern.

C strings are scanned or transferred from one to the other using loops that halt on finding either the target or the null terminator. As long as you are sure that the strings are null-terminated i.e. they are strings your program created, then this is usually not a problem. Where the problems start is when your program accepts input from another source – a user say or data via an input port or network.

In such cases it is better to use the similar related functions, the safe string functions, starting with the prefix `strn` – where the n signifies the use of an additional parameter an upper bound on the number of chars to process.
For example:

```
char myString1[10] = "abc";
char myString2[] = "def";
strncat(myString1, myString2,3);
```

This is the same as the previous `strcat` example and the result is the same, i.e. "abcdef" followed by a null terminator. The important difference is that at most 3 chars will be copied from `myString2` even if it isn't null-terminated. Notice that the destination, `myString1` in this case, is always null-terminated and so it needs to have space for n+1 characters from `myString2`. The only thing that can go wrong with this function call is if `myString1` doesn't have enough space, and as you know it has to have at least n+1 free elements you should be able to ensure this.

If you are trying to assign one string to another then don't use `strcpy`, which is fine for assigning a string literal, instead use `strncpy`:

```
char myString1[10]="abc";
char myString2[10]="def";
strncpy(myString1,myString2,10);
```

While there is no danger of array overrun it is possible that `myString1` will not have a null terminator if `myString2` doesn't have one or if it beyond the 10 char limit.

The other `strn` functions work in the same way and you can use them to avoid string overflow.

Buffer Overflow

Usually the discussion of avoiding string or more generally array or buffer overflow ends at this point, but in the real world things are more complex.

When programming in C you need to be aware of where array data comes from. In general, the arrays and strings that you create and consume are safe enough because you know their size and can ensure that they are null-terminated where necessary. This means that you can use null-terminated string functions if you want to. This includes any functions you might write - you don't have to further protect a function that you know only you are going to use and in a responsible manner.

Where things get dangerous is when data is generated externally – user input, network data, file data, or anything that is not originated by your program. In this case you have to put an upper limit on the number of items of data you are prepared to accept. This usually means using `strn` functions as opposed to `str` functions and more generally specifying array sizes. It also means that you have to remember to check that an array access is within the array bounds for every access – this is inefficient but safe.

Of course, in the real world implementing such strategies is always much harder. For example, consider the network data problem. You set up an array to accept data from a device or a service which normally sends you 500 bytes. However, you have no guarantee that network problems or exceptional circumstances might not force it to send 750 bytes or more. In an ideal world you would simply allocate an array so huge that overrunning it was unlikely – you would still have to check that it wasn't overrun, however. In the real world you generally can't afford that sort of memory allocation, especially on small devices. So what can you do?

In most case the best solution is to divide the transaction into packets of data. Read in the first 500 bytes, process it and see if there is any more. In this way you can safely reuse the 500 bytes you have allocated to the array and still not miss any data that goes beyond this limit. Of course, any processing that you do has to be fast enough so that you can carry on reading the next 500 bytes without missing any data or even aborting the connection due to a timeout.

The exact details of implementing the repeated use of a small buffer to read in large amounts of data varies according to how the data transfer protocol works and what is to be done with the data, but a for loop and a test of the end of the data is generally what is required. In the case of limited resources it is often necessary to trade code for memory.

Convert to String - sprintf

You already know how to convert a bit pattern to a human readable string using `printf`. The string function `sprintf` – string print formatted – works in exactly the same way but it returns a string rather than printing the string.

All of the format strings work with `sprintf` the only real difference is that it returns a string.

For example:

```
sprintf(myString,"The result = %10d",1234);
```

If you are worried about the function returning a string, notice that you have to supply a string that has enough storage to store the result. The example really should be:

```
char myString[25];
sprintf(myString,"The result = %10d",1234);
```

The result is a formatted string exactly as you see printed stored in myString. You might not see the full reason for sprintf at the moment, but it is very useful if you are working with any sort of non-standard display and need to get a character representation to send to it. More generally you can use it as a way of converting any data type into a string which can be further processed. There are also some simpler functions which convert particular data types into strings without any format specification. See later.

Input – Buffer Problems

It is also worth knowing that the scanf function will read in a string from standard input device, usually the keyboard, using a format string that is the same as printf. The user is expected to supply the data that would otherwise come from the variables in a printf.

For example, to get the user to enter some characters as a string you would use:

```
scanf("%s",myString);
```

Most introductions to C explain how this can be used to get input and show examples that often don't work as expected. There are a number of significant problems with scanf and indeed with trying to get input from a user.

The biggest problem is that if you are running C under a full operating system then the input from the keyboard will generally be buffered. That is, as the user types on the keyboard the character codes are stored in a buffer even if you aren't using the input. When scanf is used in your program it reads from the buffer rather than interacting with the keyboard directly.

It is also worth knowing that your output sent to the display device is also buffered and it only appears on the screen when you send a newline or when the program terminates. This too often causes problems as you wonder why what you have "printf-ed" to the screen isn't appearing.

Consider the following simple program:

```
char myString[25];
printf("What is your name");
scanf("%s",myString);
printf("Hi %s",myString);
```

The intent is that the user sees the "What is your name" prompt and then types a reply. Under most systems, including Windows and Linux, the program just seems to hang. The reason is that the message goes into the output buffer and just sits there. If there is nothing in the input buffer the scanf also just waits for something to be typed. The user has no indication that they should type anything. If they do type anything then nothing happens until they press return once or perhaps twice and then you see the question and the answer as the program comes to an end and the output buffer is flushed.

There are many ways to solve the problem, but by far the most common is to use the system specific fflush(stdin) and fflush(stdout) which empty the buffers concerned under many operating systems.

So if you try the program using `fflush`:

```
char myString[25];
printf("What is your name");
fflush(stdout);
fflush(stdin);
scanf("%s",myString);
printf("Hi %s",myString);
```

you will see the message appear, and you will be able to type in a name. However, you might not see what you type and you might have to enter two returns to make it work.

Whether or not you see what you type depends on the console your program is using and whether or not it has echo on or off. If echo is off then you will not see what you type. Under NetBeans the internal console doesn't echo what you type. To turn echo on right-click on the project and select Properties. Under the Run tab select Standard Output for Console type. Now you will be able to see what you type in response to a `scanf`.

Another problem with using `scanf` is that the format strings fail at the first mismatch and this leaves characters in the buffer to confuse the next attempt at reading. The `%s` format specifier only reads until the first white space character, which means including spaces in names, say, causes it to stop. What is worse is that a white space doesn't stop the `scanf` reading data from the buffer – after all there might be another format specifier. Many of the format specifiers skip input characters rather than give up trying to read data.

For example:

```
scanf("%d",&number);
```

will work as expected if you type 123 return, say, but if you type something other than numbers, including a blank line, then the machine will generally just appear to hang. The reason is that `%d` will skip as many white space characters, including carriage return, until it finds some digits and a return.

There are many more "gotchas" in using `scanf` and it would take a chapter dedicated to the subject to list them all, but you can usually understand what is happening by finding out exactly what a format specifier is looking for and by remembering that you are working with a buffer.

In most cases it is better to avoid using `scanf` to get input from a user. You will often hear the advice – don't use `scanf`. In fact this is too extreme. When it comes to reading in formatted data stored in a file or stream, `scanf` can be useful. The reason is that a file or stream generally has a clear fixed format and you can tailor the `scanf` format to suit. Also if anything goes wrong you can often back up and try again.

It is also worth commenting that, for low-level applications, input from the keyboard is generally not an issue because there is no keyboard. For higher-level applications there might well be a keyboard, but generally you need some more advanced form of UI and for this you need a library or a framework – ncurses for console and Qt say for a full GUI. These generally have their own I/O functions. However, for working with keyboard input, we need an alternative method of dealing with user input.

Low-level I/O

There are a number of I/O functions that are simpler than `printf` and `scanf`:

putchar & getchar

These put and get a single char from the standard I/O streams. If you try:

```
printf("type a character ");
int c=getchar();
putchar(c);
```

then the chances are very high that you will discover that buffers are still getting in the way and you don't see the "type a character" message until after you have typed a character. The simplest fix is to use `fflush`, even if it is system-dependent:

```
printf("type a character ");
fflush(stdout);
int c=getchar();
putchar(c);
```

However, now you will discover that you have to press return after the character, once again because of the buffer. If you type "abcdef" then nothing happens till you press return, when the buffer is made available to `getchar` and a single character is removed from the buffer. You can use `getchar` again to read more of the buffer. Also notice that `getchar` and `putchar` work in terms of `int` rather than `char`.

The two functions are sometimes useful, but not as a way to dynamically interact with the keyboard as you might expect.

gets & puts

These two functions work like `getchar` and `putchar` but they work with complete C strings. For example:

```
printf("type a string ");
fflush(stdout);
char s[25];
gets(s);
puts(s);
```

As in the case of `getchar` the buffer is only used by `gets` when the user presses return when `gets` reads characters into the string until it reaches the end of the buffer. The string `s` is null-terminated and includes any `newline` used to end the input.

Notice that `gets` is dangerous in that it will accept as many characters as the user types and thus an array overflow is very possible. To avoid this problem use `fgets` instead.

fgets

The fgets function is designed to read a string from any data stream but it is the obvious alternative to the dangerous gets because it allows you to specify a maximum for the number of characters read. The safe equivalent of the previous example is:

```
printf("type a string ");
fflush(stdout);
char s[25];
fgets(s,25,stdin);
puts(s);
```

Notice that the 25 in the call to fgets means you cannot have a buffer overflow but you can stop reading data before it is complete. As with reading a general array the solution to this is to repeat the read and process each chunk until all of the data has been processed.

A Safe Way To Do Input – String Conversion

The `scanf` function is easy to use but both dangerous and unstable. Many C users when presented with this fact have in the past created their own version of `scanf` – a very complex alternative.

A much better and simple way to proceed is to use fgets to safely read in a complete line of text and then use string conversion functions to extract the data.

The string conversion functions are all of the same form:

```
strtod(string, end);
strtol(string, end, base);
strtoul(string, end, base);
```

which convert to double, long or unsigned long respectively. The string is scanned and the value built up as legal characters are encountered. The scanning stops when a character that cannot be part of a number is encountered or the end of the string. The end parameter is set to point at the location that the scan stopped so that the rest of the string can be processed. Finally, base is the numeric base to be used for the conversion, usually 10.

For example:

```
char s[]="1234.456 Some data";
char *prt;
int num=strtol(s,&prt,10);
printf("%d",num);
```

Prints 1234 and leaves prt pointing at the space before "Some data". For the moment don't worry about the use of the & in &prt, it is explained in the next chapter.

The strtol and strtoul work in the same way, converting legal characters to a value and stopping at the first non-legal character.

You might wonder why there is no strtoi or similar?

The simple answer is that there is no need as long can be reduced to int or short if the numeric value is small enough, and the same is true of unsigned long. There are some older functions atoi, atof and atol which convert a string to int, float and long respectively but don't use them as they are can overrun the string.

The atoi family of functions scan a string until they find a suitable set of characters to convert. That is:

```
atoi("the number is 123");
```

will return 123 whereas strtol stops at once on 't'. You can use the fact that ptr is the start of the string to test to see if any valid characters were found. The problem is that atoi will carry on scanning a string until it finds a valid character even if this results in it going beyond the end of the string.

The best way to do safe input from the keyboard is to use the strto functions on the string returned from fgets.

For example, suppose you want the user to input an integer and a number with a decimal point separated by a comma:

```
char myString[25];
printf("type a int,double ");
fflush(stdout);
fgets(myString,25,stdin);
char *prt;
int num1=strtol(myString,&prt,10);
printf("%d",num1);
prt++;
double num2=strtod(prt,&prt);
printf("%f",num2);
```

The `fgets` reads in a whole line from the user and it allows the user to edit the line before pressing enter. Next we use `strtol` to extract the integer digits. The scan stops at the comma and this is what `prt` is pointing at. Adding one to `prt` moves it past the comma, in a real application we need to check that the comma is there and that the floating value is next. The `strtod` extracts the floating value.

All of this is easy and safe and, if you need to get input from the keyboard, is the best approach unless you are using a library or GUI framework.

Summary

- Strings are null-terminated char arrays.

- A char is generally a single byte and it is the smallest of the integer types.

- The character code used depends on the operating system, but you can generally assume that you are working with UTF-8 restricted to a single byte which is functionally equivalent to ASCII.

- C doesn't currently handle Unicode well.

- You can initialize a string using a string literal, but you cannot assign a string literal to a string.

- Always make sure that the array has enough elements to hold the string and its null terminator. If the string has n characters the array has to have at least n+1 elements.

- A string variable is a pointer to the first element of the string and behaves like a standard array.

- There are no native string operators or functions in C but the standard library has a comprehensive set of string functions.

- All string operations work by using a for loop to scan the string and stop when it reaches the null terminator.

- If the null terminator is missing then most string operations will overrun the array.

- There are alternative safe string functions which allow you to specify the maximum number of characters to be processed. Used correctly these protect you against array overrun.

- String overflow is generally easy to control when all of the strings involved are generated by your program. Things are much more difficult when strings are input from external sources.

- Printf and sprintf can be used to convert integer and floating point types to human readable string representations.

- Operating system buffers make interactive I/O using scanf difficult.

- Scanf also has problems in terms of how it applies the format string to the input.

- In many cases the only solution is to use lower-level I/O functions to control the way the characters are converted into numeric data types.

Pointers are the construct that makes C so useful for low-level and system programming. They allow you to do things that high-level languages usually forbid or make difficult. In a sense it is the pointer that allows you to use C rather than have to resort to a machine-specific assembler. Of course, with such power comes great responsibility to not crash your program, or indeed the entire machine. It is probably the pointer and its incorrect, or careless, use that causes C to be thought of as a "dangerous" language.

In this chapter we look at the C pointer and how it relates to C's memory model.

Declaring a Pointer – The Dereference Operator

You have probably been using variables ever since you learned to program and you probably think of them as some sort of "box" that a value can be stored in. That is, when you write:

```
int myVar=123;
```

you think of myVar as in some sense "containing" or storing the value 123. In fact what is happening is the int type declaration causes the compiler to allocate two (or more) bytes and store the binary equivalent of 123 in it. From this point on the label myVar is a synonym for the address of the allocated memory location – as explained in Chapter 4 a variable is a constant pointer.

This is a subtle shift in understanding. No storage is allocated to store the address of the variable, it is just inserted into the machine code as part of the instruction. When you write:

```
int myVar;
myVar=0;
```

the compiler issues the assembler:

```
main+14: movl    $0x0,0xc(%esp)
```

This moves a value of zero into memory at 0xC relative to the current stack frame. You can see that myVar is replaced though out the program by the use of memory location 0xC in the stack frame.

Standard variables do for most things, but occasionally you need to refer to a memory location that changes during the course of the program. For this you need a pointer.

A pointer is a variable that stores the address of a memory location and it differs from a variable in that some storage is allocated to store the address.

In C you use the * or the dereference operator to indicate that a variable is a pointer.

For example:

```
int *myPointer;
```

declares myPointer as a pointer to int. Notice that no int is created by this declaration. What is created is an area of memory that can store the address of an int, and myPointer is a label that gives the address of this area. That is, myPointer is a variable that stores the address of an int.

This implies that all pointers take the same amount of memory irrespective of what they point at, as an address nearly always occupies the same number of bits.

Why then do we have to state that myPointer is a pointer to int and not something else?

After all, myPointer is just going to store an address and all addresses are the same sort of thing and occupy the same storage space. The reason is that the compiler needs to know what to do with the memory that the pointer points at.

To be more precise, the dereference operator accesses that memory that the pointer points at. That is:

```
myPointer
```

is a pointer to int and:

```
*myPointer
```

is the actual int that myPointer points at.

Once you have dereferenced a pointer you can use it as if it was the type that is the target of the pointer.

For example:

```
*myPointer=42;
```

stores 42 as an int in the memory location addressed by myPointer.

Before you rush away to try it out – this doesn't work because myPointer, as far as we have defined it, may be a pointer but it doesn't actually point at any usable memory. Declaring a pointer creates an uninitialized pointer just like declaring any variable declares an uninitialized variable.

So how can we initialize a pointer?

Initializing a Pointer – The Address Operator

The most direct, although not the most common way, to do the job is to simply assign an address to the pointer.

For example:

```
int *myPointer;
myPointer=0xFFFF;
```

where `0xFFFF` is a hexadecimal literal. You can now try and print the `int` stored at address `0xFFFF`:

```
printf("%d",*myPointer);
```

You are unlikely to see anything printed and your program should crash because there is little chance that address `0xFFFF` is within your legal address space. However, if it was, and if you are working with a small embedded system it might be, then you would see whatever bits are stored at the address interpreted as an int. There is nothing illegal about the program, but you might see a warning due to the assignment of an int to a pointer to int. To do the job properly needs a `cast` – more of which later – for the moment we can ignore the problem. Direct assignment of this sort is not commonplace, but it is essential if you need to access memory-mapped hardware. You can learn more about this in ***Applying C For The IoT With Linux*** ISBN: 978-1871962611.

So how do you get an address that is valid within your program and which refers to a valid `int`, or whatever type the pointer is to reference?

There are a number of possible answers, but the most basic is the & or address operator.

This returns the address of any variable you apply it to.

This is literally what & does – it finds the address of what you apply it to, but a much better way to think of it is as converting a type into a pointer to that type.

For example:

```
int myVar;
```

is an `int` variable but:

```
&myVar;
```

is a pointer to `int`. At a slightly lower level it is also obvious that it is the address associated with `myVar`.

To be clear, if `myVar` is a type then `&myVar` is a pointer to the type. In most cases you can interpret this as the address of `myVar`.

You can see that * and & are inverse operators. The * operator makes a type from a pointer, whereas the & operator makes a pointer from a type.

For example:

```
int myVar=42;
int *myPointer;
myPointer=&myVar;
*myPointer=123;
printf("%d",*myPointer);
```

The first declaration creates an int and sets it to 42. Keep in mind that this int is just an area of memory at an address storing the bit pattern corresponding to 42 in binary.

The second declaration creates a pointer to int which is initialized in the next instruction to the address of myVar. You can say that myPointer is now a pointer to myVar or you could say that *myPointer is the same as myVar.

The next line stores 123 in the memory pointed to by myPointer, i.e. it has the same effect as myVar=123.

Finally we print *myPointer and see 123.

Pointer beginners often have difficult in following what is going on.

If you always think that if myPointer is a pointer to an int then *myPointer is an int and if myVar is an int then &myVar is a pointer to an int, then you should find it easier.

What do the following print?

```
printf("%d \n",*myPointer);
printf("%p \n",myPointer);
printf("%p \n",&myPointer);
```

The first prints the int that is *myPointer i.e. 123, the second prints the address of *myPointer and the third prints the address of the variable myPointer. Notice the use of %p to format an address in hex. You can use %d if you want to see the address in decimal.

To summarize:

- ◆ *type* *variable declares *variable to be the *type* and hence *variable* to be a pointer to *type*.

- ◆ If *variable* is a pointer to *type*, the dereference operator makes it a type. That is, if *variable* is a pointer to *type*, *variable is the *type*.

- ◆ If *variable* is declared to be *type* then &*variable* is a pointer to *type*, i.e. an address.

- ◆ That is, * makes a type out of a pointer and & makes a pointer out of a type.

Pointers and Arrays

Being able to take the address of a variable and use a pointer to it instead of using it directly is a good illustration of how pointers work, but it isn't often useful. To be of any great use, pointers need some way of allocating memory that they can point to and that isn't just the reuse of memory already allocated to a variable.

In many cases pointers are the default way of accessing C's few data structures. In fact we have already encountered pointers in connection with arrays – a simple data structure that deserves to be encountered before the intricacies of pointers, but one that is essentially about pointers.

When you declare an array the compiler allocates a block of memory large enough to store the entire array and creates a pointer to store the address of the first element, i.e. the start of the allocated block.

That is:

```
int myArray[20];
```

reserves enough storage for 20 ints, i.e. `sizeof(int) *20` bytes and `myArray` refers to the address of the first element.

In most cases, `myArray` behaves as if it was a pointer to `int`, but there are some subtle differences. The first is that `myArray` is more like a label rather than a full pointer. When you use `myArray[0]`, for example, the compiler treats `myArray` as a constant pointer, i.e. an address, which it inserts into the machine code. A true pointer is a memory location that stores the address.

What this means in practice is that while you can use `myArray` as if it was a pointer, you cannot assign a new address to it and it is not a `lvalue`, unless you convert it into a true pointer.

For example, if you try:

```
int myVar=42;
int myArray[20];
myArray=&myVar;
```

you will see an error that is something like:

```
error: assignment to expression with array type
```

An array name is an expression of array type and not a pointer.

However, you can create a pointer to do the same job as an array variable:

```
int *myPointer;
int myArray[20];
myPointer=myArray;
printf("%d \n",myPointer[0]);
```

In this case we have assigned the address of the start of the array to a pointer and then used it as if it was an array – how is this last part possible?

Pointer Arithmetic

Suppose you have a pointer to a block of memory that contains repeated elements of the same type. For example, an `int` array is just a block of memory that is regarded as being one `int` followed by another. In this case the first `int` pointed to by the array name or an equivalent pointer.

That is, after:

```
int *myPointer;
int myArray[20];
myPointer=myArray;
```

`myPointer` references the first `int` in the array and

```
printf("%d \n",*myPointer);
```

prints the contents of the first element, i.e. `myArray[0]`.

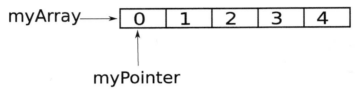

Where is the second element?

The answer is, displaced in memory from the start of the array by whatever the size of an int is.

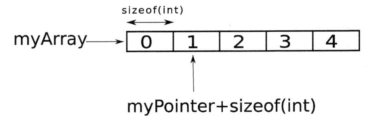

That is, the address of the second element i.e. `myArray[1]` is given by
`myPointer+sizeof(int);`

By the same argument the third element, i.e. `myArray[2]` is given by:
`myPointer+sizeof(int)*2;`

In general, the address of the Ith element is:
`myPointer+sizeof(int)*I;`

This is the reason that C arrays start from zero index. If you wanted an array to start from index one you would need to subtract one from I in the above expression – not difficult but starting at zero is natural given the way elements are stored offset from the start of the array.

This calculation is so standard for pointers that C makes it the default and:

```
myPointer+I;
```

is taken to mean not +I but +sizeof(int)*I.

This is pointer arithmetic, and addition and subtraction are all you can do with pointers. Adding one adds sizeof(type) to the pointer and subtracting one reduces it by sizeof(type). You can also use ++ and - - but that's all – no multiply or divide.

If you have a pointer to the start of an array, and it is a pointer to the type that the array stores, then the Ith element is addressed by:

```
myPointer+I;
```

and this is equivalent to the address of:

```
myArray[I];
```

In fact the [] array indexing operator is exactly equivalent to pointer arithmetic. That is:

```
myArray[I];
```

is the same as:

```
*(myArray+I);
```

and:

```
*(myPointer+I);
```

Notice that there is still the subtle difference in using a pointer or an array variable in that myArray+I is evaluated as a constant address plus I whereas myPointer+I is the contents of a variable, i.e. a memory location, plus I.

Although these examples have used int as the element type, the same things work for any element type with sizeof returning the size of the element. Notice that an array variable is slightly faster as it produces simpler machine code, but the difference is small.

Although there are differences between array variables and pointers, you can simplify things by always thinking of a pointer as if it was an array of elements. If the pointer is to a single variable then think of it as a single-element array.

Functions and Pointers

Pointers are particularly important for implementing functions that can work with data structures and for functions needing to return values via parameters. We have already met an example of this in the way passing an array variable as a parameter allows the function to change elements of the array. This works because the array is passed as a pointer and this is a general principle. If you want a function to have access to a data structure and to be able to modify that data structure then pass a pointer to it into the function.

To pass a pointer into a function you simply declare the parameter's type in the usual way:

```
void myFunc(int *myPointer){
```

Within the function the pointer is used in the normal way with the dereference and address operators.

For example, to pass an int into a function so that its value can be changed we have to pass a pointer to int:

```
void myFunc(int *myPointer){
     *myPointer=42;
}
```

Notice that the parameter is declared to be a pointer to int. The assignment is to the dereferenced pointer, i.e. to the int that the pointer references. When you first see this sort of code there is tendency to think that the parameter is *myPointer, partly because of the way the function declaration looks and partly because in the program the parameter tends to be used as *myPointer. In fact, the parameter is myPointer and the function declaration says that *myPointer is an int so myPointer must be a pointer to int. Similarly, the assignment is to an int, the int that myPointer references.

You can try this function very easily:

```
int myVar=0;
myFunc(&myVar);
printf("%d \n",myVar);
```

and you will see that myVar now contains 42. Notice the use of &myVar to pass a pointer to int which is what the function parameter is.

Passing data into a function is the main purpose of parameters. The return value of a function is the intended way of getting results out of a function. Using a parameter to pass a result back to the calling program is generally not a good idea, but it is fairly standard practice in C. It would be much better to write the example function as:

```
int myFunc(){
     return 42;
}
```

then the function would be called as:

```
myVar=myFunc();
```

If you need to return a single result from a function, use return not a pointer parameter.

If you need to return more than a single result then consider returning a data structure which contains all of the results. For example, if you need a function that computes the maximum and minimum of an int array then return an array that contains the max and min or better return a struct – see later. The problem with this is that the function has to create the data structure and pack it with the values which then have to be unpacked by the calling program. However, it is often worth the extra work for the stability this approach brings.

Pointer parameters are more or less unavoidable when you need to pass a data structure. For large data structures it is not efficient to create a copy for the function to work on and so pass-by-value is not a reasonable approach. Passing a pointer, by value, to the function is the only reasonable approach and this is what happens when you pass an array as discussed in the previous chapters.

The example given in the Chapter 8 now makes more sense in terms of pointers:

```
int sum(int myArray[],int n){
    int total=0;
    for(int i=0;i<n;i++){
        total=total+myArray[i];
    }
    return total;
}
```

The array expression passed to the function "decays to a pointer".

An explicit pointer version of the sum function, which is the same in every respect, would be:

```
int sum(int *myArray,int n){
    int total=0;
    for(int i=0;i<n;i++){
        total=total+*(myArray+i);
    }
    return total;
}
```

and you could call it using an explicit pointer using:

```
int myArray[1000]={1,2,3};
int total=sum(&myArray[0],1000);
printf("%d",total);
```

The covering up of the way pointers are used in passing arrays is a simplification for the beginner, but if you are to master C and understand some of the subtle mistakes it is possible to make, then you need to know how things actually work in detail.

Notice that, as strings are just `char` arrays, the same ideas apply without modification.

The best practice adopted by most modern languages is the principle of immutability. Data structures are passed to functions using a slightly higher-level abstractions of the pointer. They are passed by reference, but in most cases the default is that the data structure is immutable – that is, it cannot be changed. Notice that the sum function does not change the array it is passed, it simply accesses its elements. If a function does want to change a data structure then it creates a whole new data structure. This approach is safer from the point of view of bugs and it allows easier concurrency because there is no chance that two threads will attempt to change the same data structure. In C, however, immutability is the exception and it is a matter of understanding the hardware and the available resources whether or not it is a good idea.

Allocating Memory

We still have a problem of how to allocate memory for a pointer to reference. At the moment the only solution we have is to create arrays and this suits many situations, but it isn't particularly flexible. For example, how can you extend the idea of an array to something that can change its size? There is also the small matter that functions cannot create data structures which persist beyond their lifetime, i.e. a function cannot pass a data structure it has created to the calling program.

The solution to all of these problems and more is the `malloc` function. This is a function, implemented by the operating system, that will allocate memory from the heap. In most, if not all, modern machine architectures a program has two types of memory available to it – stack and heap, see Chapter 7. To recap:

- The stack is often referred to as automatic or auto memory because it is what a program gets to use by default. For example, any local variables that you create within a function are allocated on the stack. It is in the nature of stack memory that it can only be accessed by the parts of the program that it was allocated to. So only a function can access the local variables it creates.

- Heap memory is accessible from any part of a program, irrespective of what allocated it. This is one of the things that makes it useful. The other useful characteristic of the heap is that you can reallocate or deallocate any memory you are using. This makes it very powerful and very general.

The way C has access to the heap makes it possible to do almost anything, but as before with great power comes great responsibly and if pointers are regarded as dangerous, pointers plus heap access is potentially the work of the devil.

Other languages don't allow direct access to the heap and in return they manage it for you by allocating and deallocating as needs be. This is generally called memory management and the act of automatically deallocating memory that is no longer in use is called garbage collection or GC. The C language does not have an automatic GC – you are C's garbage collector. This is often said to be a huge disadvantage of C because not doing garbage collection properly is the cause of many bugs and memory leaks. It is possible, in C, to not free memory correctly and so slowly, and sometimes not so slowly, use up all of the memory that a machine has.

All this said – if you are going to write programs that are in complete control of the machine and which are maximally efficient then doing your own memory management is almost your only option. There are many simple cases where manually allocating memory is easy, controllable and essential.

The basic `malloc` function call is:

```
pointer=malloc(size);
```

This returns a pointer to a contiguous block of memory of size bytes allocated from the heap. What you do with this memory is entirely up to you. If the machine has run out of memory then `malloc` returns a pointer set to NULL. A null pointer is generally, but not always, a pointer with the address of zero. In most machine architectures memory location zero is off limits to ordinary programs and so a null pointer doesn't reference any memory and any attempt to dereference it generally crashes the program. So in all cases you need to test that the pointer returned by `malloc` isn't NULL. This is easy:

```
if(pointer==NULL) do something about running out of memory;
```

what is harder is working out what to do about running out of memory.

The memory that you are allocated is uninitialized and if the operating system or machine doesn't do something about it, then what is stored in it is whatever the last program left in it. Having uninitialized memory is usually the most efficient but if you do want the memory initialized you can use:

```
pointer=calloc(size);
```

which works in the same way as `malloc` but it zeros the block of memory.

The only other memory allocation functions you need to know are:

```
free(pointer);
```

which returns that block of memory pointed to by the pointer to the heap, and:

```
newpointer=realloc(pointer, newsize);
```

which attempts to change the size of the block of memory pointed to by the `pointer` to `newsize`. If the reallocation fails then it returns NULL.

For example, to allocate a block of 100 bytes, reallocate it to 200 bytes and then free the memory:

```
void *pointer=malloc(100);
printf("%p\n",pointer);
pointer=realloc(pointer, 200);
printf("%p\n",pointer);
free(pointer);
```

In most cases you will find that the start of the block changes on reallocation, i.e. the reallocation isn't necessarily done "in place", and it is usual for the block to be destroyed and recreated at a new location. The system will generally do this in a more efficient way than you could by allocating a new block, copying the data and freeing the original block.

It is worth noting at this early stage that the `free` function will only free the block of memory that the supplied pointer references. This might seem obvious, but if the block of memory has been used to store other pointers then the memory that they point at will not be freed. Each time you allocate memory you have to free it separately. Obvious though this is now, when you have used `malloc` to construct a complicated data structure it is very easy to think that freeing the memory that it occupies frees all of the memory associated with it. There is one last unexplained detail - what does `void` mean as a pointer type? The answer will shortly be revealed.

Casting Pointers

Now we come to a very important topic – casting pointers.

A pointer is an address of a block of memory and you can either regard that block of memory as typed or untyped. The difference comes down to the type of the pointer. If you recall, the type of a pointer modifies how pointer arithmetic is done and how the compiler treats what the pointer references.

That is a cast applied to a pointer changes the type of what it points at.

A raw block of memory that is just treated as such, a block of bytes if you like, needs an untyped pointer. This is declared as a pointer to `void`:

```
void *myPointer;
```

As mentioned earlier, C tends to use the term void for anything that isn't something. A void pointer can point at anything and the compiler will not assume anything about it, and hence pointer arithmetic on a void pointer isn't allowed. Note: some compilers do allow, or can be set to allow void pointer arithmetic.

If you want to treat a block of memory as a set of bytes and do pointer arithmetic then the simplest thing to do is to use a pointer to char. When you use malloc it returns a pointer to void – after all it has no idea what you are allocating the memory for. In most cases, to use the memory you need to cast the pointer to void to something else.

For example:

```
char *myPointer=(char*)malloc(100);
```

allocates 100 bytes of memory and sets myPointer to its address. The pointer to void is cast to a pointer to char so after this you can use myPointer as if is was an array of char or as a raw pointer to char complete with pointer arithmetic. Note that C99 doesn't require the explicit cast and will perform the cast automatically. However, it is still good practice to write the cast to explicitly indicate what you intend.

For example, both:

```
myPointer[50]='A';
```

and:

```
*(myPointer+50)='A';
```

work perfectly. This is how you convert a block of allocated memory into something like an array of any type you care to use.

It is usual to express the size of the block of memory to be allocated in terms of the size of the proposed elements. That is, you would write:

```
char *myPointer=(char*)malloc(100*sizeof(char));
```

to allocate an "array" of 100 char. The same works for any type of element:

```
type pointer=malloc(n*sizeof(type))
```

and is the pointer equivalent of declaring an array of n elements.

The real advantage of allocating memory on the heap is that it is dynamic. For example, if you want to create an array that can change its size you need to write something like:

```
char *myCharArray=(char *)malloc(100);
for(int i=0;i<100;i++){
    myCharArray[i]=i;
}
```

This sets up an array of 100 elements on the heap and sets each element to its position value in the array using array notation. Now suppose the array is too small and you want to add another 100 elements. All you need to do is realloc:

```
myCharArray=(char *)realloc(myCharArray,200);
for(int i=100;i<200;i++){
    myCharArray[i]=i;
}
```

Notice that we have set the new elements to their position in the array – but as this is only an 8-bit element this "rolls over" at 127 to negative values according to two's-complement representation.

You can check the contents of the array using:

```
for(int i=0;i<200;i++){
    printf("%d\n",myCharArray[i]);
}
```

Notice that the system has copied the existing elements to the new block of memory – this is usually implemented more efficiently than you could write the same process in C.

Type Punning

For low-level programming the need to manipulate the bytes that make up a more complex representation is very common. One longstanding way of doing the job, especially in programs that target a particular fixed architecture, is to use type cast punning that is to use pointers of different types to the same memory.

For example, suppose you want to use the block of memory to store either chars or ints, then all you have to do is create two appropriate pointers:

```
char *myCharPointer = (char*) malloc(100);
int *myIntPointer = (int*) myCharPointer;
```

Now you have two pointers that point to the same block of memory, but one treats it as an array of char and the other an array of int.

It may be longstanding and very common, but it is also undefined behavior in C99 and C11, where if you need to treat a bit pattern as different types you should use a union – see Chapter 11. However, this said, there are lots of C programmers who find type punning to be perfectly acceptable and continue to use it.

What practical use is type punning?

For example, suppose a device, stream or other source of data sends you an integer value as four separate bytes. Then you could put the data together using something like:

```
char *myCharPointer = (char*) malloc(100);
myCharPointer[0]=1;
myCharPointer[1]=2;
myCharPointer[2]=3;
myCharPointer[3]=4;

int *myIntPointer = (int*) myCharPointer;
printf("%d \n",myIntPointer[0]);
```

where in this case the input bytes have been set by assignment for simplicity to 1,2,3,4 whereas in general these values would be arbitrary. The final printf displays the four bytes as an int. Notice that what actual value you get depends on the order that the bytes are used to build the int. If the lower order bytes are stored first then we have little-endian order. If the high-order bytes are stored first then we have big-endian order – see Chapter 12.

Once you have seen this sort of technique you will find many uses for it and will avoid writing programs that involve time-wasting packing and unpacking as data is moved around and modified by expressions to build up the value required. What you need to understand is that in C data is just a bit pattern and how this is interpreted is controlled by type and casts to type. Notice that this works with local variables as well as allocated memory.

For example:

```
int myVar;
char *myCharPointer = (char*) &myVar;
myCharPointer[0]=1;
myCharPointer[1]=2;
myCharPointer[2]=3;
myCharPointer[3]=4;
printf("%d \n",myVar);
```

This casts the pointer to int obtained using & to a pointer to char. The pointer to char looks like a char or byte array and this is how we make use of it in the following assignments. When you print myVar you will discover that its value has been changed.

The same technique can be used to pass data of one type when a function is expecting another. For example, a common task is to form the sum or some other complex expression of say four bytes of data:

```
int sumHash(char bytes[4]){
    int sum=0;
    for(int i=0;i<4;i++){
        sum+=bytes[i];
    }
    return sum;
}
```

In practice, the calculation of the "hash" would be much more complicated than just summing the values in each byte, but the principle is the same.

Now suppose that you would like to compute the hash on a single int. You might start to think that the thing to do is unpack each byte of the int into a char array of the correct size, but it is much simpler to use pointer casting:

```
int myVar=12345678;
int result=sumHash((char *) &myVar);
printf("%d\n",result);
```

The function is expecting a char array, which is the same as a pointer to char. In the call to the function the parameter we want to pass is an int variable. To convert this to pointer to char we first convert it to pointer to int using & and then cast it to pointer to char. The function treats the four bytes occupied by the int as a char[4] array.

As long as the data you want to work with is suitably arranged in memory, then you can generally treat it as any type that suits the occasion. Even when it looks as if pointer casting cannot help, it usually can. For example, consider the problem of passing an int to a rewritten sumHash function:

```
int sumHash(char byte1,char byte2,char byte3,char byte4){
    int sum=byte1+byte2+byte3+byte4;
    return sum;
}
```

Now the function needs each byte supplied as a separate parameter. Surely we now have to work on unpacking the int into four separate bytes?

The best solution is to remember that pointers are arrays:

```
int result=sumHash(((char *) &myVar)[0], ((char *) &myVar)[1],
                   ((char *) &myVar)[2],((char *) &myVar)[3]);
```

A clearer way to write this is:

```
char *temp=(char *) &myVar;
int result=sumHash(temp[0], temp[1], temp[2],temp[3]);
```

Once you have a pointer to data you can access any part of it using indexing or pointer arithmetic.

To cast a variable to another type:

1. use & to obtain a pointer to the type
2. cast the pointer to the type to a pointer to the new type
3. do any pointer arithmetic that is necessary
4. dereference the pointer to obtain the type

For example, to obtain the second byte of `myVar`:

1. get a pointer to the type `&myVar`
2. cast to the new type `(char*)&myVar`
3. do pointer arithmetic `((char*)&myVar)+1`
4. dereference to obtain the type `*(((char*)&myVar)+1)`

You can usually combine steps 3 and 4 `((char*)&myVar)[1]`

Type Punning and Undefined Behavior

As stated in the previous section, type cast punning isn't architecture-independent and the C89, C99 and C11 standards introduced a strict aliasing policy. When you first encounter it type punning seems safe enough, but there are lots of ways that it can go wrong.

For example, suppose a machine architecture demands that an int and a byte have to be aligned on a 16-bit word – that is their addresses have to be a multiple of 16. Now consider what happens if you use type punning to access the second byte of an int. In this case the address of the byte would not be a multiple of 16 and your program might crash due to an invalid address. As far as I know no modern machine architecture is this inflexible, but it could happen and similar problems arise with more complex data structures.

This again highlights the conflict between the programmers who regard C as always targeting a specific architecture, in which case type punning is fine, or as a machine-independent language, in which case type punning is not fine at all.

Strict aliasing demands that if pointers reference the same memory then their types are compatible. Essentially this means that the types have to be effectively the same and so it rules out casting being used for type punning.

Many of the pointer casts in the examples break strict aliasing and hence are undefined behavior. But in practice type cast punning is very commonly used in low-level programs that target particular machine architectures and nearly all C compilers allow it unless you set an optimization level greater than the default.

If you want GCC to flag such errors you need to include the command line options:

```
-fstrict-aliasing -Wstrict-aliasing
```

What can you do if you want to avoid the threat of undefined behavior? One common approach is to find out how to turn strict aliasing off in the compiler you are using. For GCC including the option:

```
-fno-strict-aliasing
```

turns off strict aliasing restrictions.

As already stated, the best alternative is to use a union – see Chapter 11. This approach is allowed in C99 and C11, but it isn't allowed in C++ which is why you will sometimes be told that you can't do it in C.

Another alternative is to use the memcpy function which works like strcpy, but with any blocks of memory not just strings. This will copy the bits from one type to another and doesn't care that they are different types.

For example:

```
float pi = 3.14;
int tempint;
memcpy(&tempint,&pi,sizeof(tempint));
printf("%d,\n",tempint);
```

copies the bits in the first four bytes of the float into the int and achieves the type punning without violating strict alias rules.

Of course this is less efficient than type cast punning, but it is claimed that the compiler will notice it and remove the copy operation. That is the compiler automatically notices that what you are doing is equivalent to type punning and makes use of it to implement your code.

As Linus Torvalds commented after a strict alias problem was uncovered:

> *Why do you think the kernel uses "-fno-strict-aliasing"?*
>
> *The gcc people are more interested in trying to find out what can be allowed by the c99 specs than about making things actually work. The aliasing code in particular is not even worth enabling, it's just not possible to sanely tell gcc when some things can alias.*

There is a very real sense in which the low-level C programmer is at war with the compiler creators.

Returning an Array from a Function

Now that we know how to allocate memory on the heap so that it remains available until it is explicitly freed, you can see how to allow a function to create and return an array or other data structure.

Consider the function we attempted to create in Chapter 8:

```
int *zero() {
    int myArray[10];
    for (int i = 0; i < 10; i++) {
        myArray[i] = 0;
    }
    return myArray;
}
```

The idea is that this creates a zeroed array of ten elements. Its problem is that it returns a pointer to the array, but the array is a local variable which is destroyed as soon as the function returns. The calling program doesn't get a pointer to an array of ints, but a pointer into a block of memory that was an array of ints before it was freed.

The solution to this sort of problem is to use malloc:

```
int *zero() {
    int *myArray=(int*)malloc(10*sizeof(int));
    for (int i = 0; i < 10; i++) {
        myArray[i] = 0;
    }
    return myArray;
}
```

The only difference is that we explicitly use a pointer and use malloc to create the block of memory it references. As the memory persists after the function terminates, everything works.

In general, if you want to return an array from a function you need to create it using malloc. The same is true of other data structures which use reference semantics and are usually allocated as local variables. The big problem is freeing the memory when the calling program no longer needs it. Whose responsibility is it to free the memory, the function or the calling program? You can argue that the function created the array and so should free it, but how does the function know that the calling program has finished with it? Equally, you can argue that the calling program owns the array and so it should free it, but does the calling program know that it owns the array and that it has to free it? The usual compromise is that functions don't create arrays in this way. Instead they ask the calling program to create the array that is passed to them and then free the array when it is finished with.

Is int* a Type?

This section is aimed at C programmers who have learned about pointers the hard way. If you are fully happy with reasoning like - *myVar is an int so myVar is a pointer to int, skip this section or read it to find out what mistakes you could have made.

When you are first learning C, or C++ for that matter, you generally encounter something like:

```
int myint;
```

right at the start of your journey to be a programmer. You, correctly, think of this as declaring an integer variable myint and int is the type of myint.

Soon after this is generalized to:

```
int myint, myotherint;
```

which you think of as declaring two integer variables.

This results in the pattern:

```
type variable,variable, variable, ... ,lastvariable;
```

being learned.

However, at about the same time or soon after you learn all of this, you also learn that you have to declare a pointer something like:

```
int* myintpointer;
```

This declares a pointer to an integer type and there is a tendency to think that int* is a type - a pointer to int.

As a result the next step is to try something like:

```
int* myintpointer, mysecondintpointer;
```

which clearly, by the slightly wrong rules we have inferred, declares two pointers to int. Of course, you quickly discover that this is not the case and what you have declared is a pointer to int, i.e. an int* and an int. This is very strange.

Beginners are often told to just treat the declaration of a pointer differently from everything else using something like:

> "the asterisk binds to the variable not the type"

- and I have no idea what this means.

As we have stressed earlier the simplest way to think about it is not to think in terms of type at all, but consider the dereferencing operator always acting as the dereferencing operator.

That is, when you write:

```
int *myintpointer;
```

This is a declaration that `*myintpointer` is an `int` and hence `myintpointer` is a pointer to `int` so that it can be dereferenced to an `int`.

You don't have think about the dereferencing operator in any way that is different in a declaration - the declaration is simply giving the type of the variable after it has been dereferenced.

Now you can work out what:

```
int *myvar1, myvar2;
```

means without any need to invoke special cases. Declarations are still always of the form:

```
type variable, variable;
```

only now you can apply allowed operators to the variables before they are assigned their type.

In other words:

```
int *myvar1, myvar2;
```

declares that `*myvar1` is an `int` and `myvar2` is an `int`.

This is what the explanation that "the asterisk binds to the variable" is trying to tell the beginner, but not quite succeeding.

You can, of course, write things like:

```
int myvar1,*myvar2, myvar3,*myvar4;
```

and so on, and all of the things you are declaring are `int`s, but two of them are only `int`s after dereferencing.

This also brings us to expressions like:

```
int **myvar;
```

Now we know it is clear that this is stating that `**myvar` is an `int`. So `*myvar` has to be a pointer to `int` and `myvar` has to be a pointer to a pointer to an `int` and yes such things are useful – see later.

And, of course, we can now write things like:

```
int *myvar1, myvar2, **myvar3;
```

and so on and know that they are all `int`s, but only after the indicated number of dereferencing.

Pointers to Functions

As well as creating pointers to data you can create pointers to functions. This might seem like a strange idea but function pointers are both useful and lead on to more sophisticated ideas. Indeed, function pointers can be used to create an object-oriented flavor of C.

At a more basic level a pointer is just the address of some data and a function pointer is just the address of some data that happens to be a function. The new element in defining a function pointer is that you have to use the function prototype notation to define the type of the pointer. That is, a function pointer is a pointer to a function that has a particular set of parameters and a particular return type. C forces you to specify these things so that the compiler can check that you are calling the function correctly.

For example, consider the simple function:

```
int sum(int a, int b){return a+b;};
```

This has a prototype:

```
int sum(int,int);
```

To define a pointer to this function type we follow the same basic pattern:

```
int (*psum)(int,int);
```

At first this looks strange.

What is being declared?

The declaration says that *psum is a function of type int (int,int), i.e. it takes two ints as parameters and returns an int. If *psum is such a function type then psum must be a pointer to that function type. Notice that any declaration that includes a parameter list is a function and the brackets around *psum are needed because of the priority of the dereference operator.

Once you have the pointer you can initialize it:

```
psum=&sum;
```

and after this you can call it:

```
int result=(*psum)(1,2);
```

Notice that brackets are needed to make sure that the dereference operator is applied to psum and not to psum(1,2). The logic is as always – psum is a pointer to a function, *psum is a function and (1,2) calls it with the parameters.

Declarations of pointers to functions often results in something that looks complicated and difficult to understand. If you read it as a standard function declaration and only then apply the dereference operator, things should be easy.

Pointers to Pointers

A pointer can reference almost anything and so a pointer can reference another pointer. This sounds mind boggling, but it is very simple as long as you keep working with the dereference operator.

For example:

```
int **myPointer2;
```

states clearly that **myPointer2 is an int. This means that *myPointer has to be a pointer to int and in turn myPointer has to be a pointer to that, i.e. a pointer to a pointer to int.

Initializing and generally working with pointers to pointers, and even more complicated things, is relatively easy if you also keep in mind that & creates a pointer to what it is applied to.

So, for example:

```
int myInt=42;
int **myPointer2;
myPointer2=&myInt;
```

is clearly wrong because &myInt is a pointer to int and myPointer2 is a pointer to a pointer to int.

A correct initialization is:

```
int myInt=42;
int **myPointer2;
int *myPointer1=&myInt;
myPointer2=&myPointer1;
```

Notice you cannot simply double up the & into an expression like &&myInt because an address is a pointer, but an address doesn't have an address unless it is stored in a variable, i.e. a pointer.

You may be thinking that pointers to pointers are something that you need only very occasionally, however, you have already encountered a major use without really noticing. Any two-dimensional array involves a pointer to a pointer. The array name is a pointer to an array of pointers.

Earlier it was stated that you can make things conceptually simpler by always thinking of a pointer as an array. If it points to a single data type then it is a one-dimensional array. This can be extended to pointers to pointers, which can be thought of as arrays of arrays i.e. two-dimensional arrays. Similarly pointers to pointers to pointers can be thought of as an array of arrays of arrays i.e. a three dimensional structure. There are differences between arrays and pointers, but thinking in this way at least gives you a start on understanding what is going on.

For example:

```
int myarray[10][10];
```

declares a two-dimensional array of 10 rows by 10 columns. The array variable myarray is a constant pointer to an array of pointers, i.e. it is a pointer to a pointer. The array of pointers are pointers to int, i.e. a one-dimensional array.

For example:

```
int myArray[4][4]={{0,1,2,3},{0,1,2,3},{0,1,2,3},{0,1,2,3}};
int *mycol=&myArray;
```

sets mycol, a pointer to int, to the first column of the array and you can now print an element of that column using:

```
printf("%d\n",mycol[0]);
```

Another way of declaring a two-dimensional array is:

```
int **myArray;
```

but, of course, now no storage is allocated for it and to set the array up you would need to use malloc.

It is instructive to see how this would be done.

First we need to allocate the array of pointers to the columns:

```
int **myArray = malloc(10 * sizeof (int*));
```

Notice that myArray is a pointer to the block of memory returned by malloc but that block of memory is in turn to be regarded as an array of pointers.

Next we have to allocate the memory required for each column:

```
for (int i = 0; i < 10; i++) {
    myArray[i] = malloc(10 * sizeof (int));
}
```

or using pointer notation:

```
for (int i = 0; i < 10; i++) {
    *(myArray+i) = malloc(10 * sizeof (int));
}
```

which is perhaps easier to understand.

Following this we can use myArray as a two-dimensional array.

For example, using array notation:

```
for (int i = 0; i < 10; i++) {
    for (int j = 0; j < 10; j++) {
        myArray[i][j] = i*j;
    }
}
for (int i = 0; i < 10; i++) {
    for (int j = 0; j < 10; j++) {
        printf("%d\n", myArray[i][j]);
    }
}
```

Notice that building the array in this way gives us some flexibility. For example, you don't have to make each column the same size. This idea is more useful when you are creating a one-dimensional array of strings, say, which vary in length.

The best example of this is the `main` program and its parameters:

```
int main(int argc, char** argv)
```

You have been using this form of `main` since the very first hello world example and it has a pointer to a pointer as its second parameter. The first parameter is easy - it is just an `int` that gives you the number of command line parameters that have been passed to main by the operating system. The second parameter looks intimidating, but it is easy to understand by applying what we know about the dereference operator.

It is clear that `**argv` is a `char`, despite the unhelpful spacing produced by NetBeans. This means `*argv` is a pointer to `char`. Another way of saying pointer to `char` is an array of `char` or a string. So `**argv` is a pointer to a string and hence it is an array of strings.

This means we could write main as:

```
int main(int argc, char *argv[])
```

You might think that you can write it as:

```
int main(int argc, char argv[][])
```

but this doesn't work because C demands that you supply the dimension of a two-dimensional array when used as a parameter. Thus the pointer, or pointer to a pointer, notation is unavoidable.

The `argc` parameter gives us how many strings are in the array and by convention `argv[0]` is the name of the program, `argv[1]` is the first command line parameter and `argv[argc-1]` gives the final command line parameter.

For example:

```
int main(int argc, char** argv) {
    for(int i=0;i<argc;i++){
        printf("%s\n",argv[i]);
    }
    return (EXIT_SUCCESS);
}
```

Even if you don't want to use pointers to pointers in sophisticated data structures, you have to master them if you want to use multi-dimensional arrays, and most importantly arrays of strings, and pass them to functions as parameters.

Immutability

As introduced earlier immutability of data structures is fast becoming the norm for many languages. For example, in both Python and Java strings are immutable and cannot be changed. Most programmers in these languages use strings without realizing that they are immutable and seem to change them without any worries. The trick is that immutable strings aren't modified but are recreated.

C doesn't really provide facilities to create immutable data structures. No matter how hard you try, there is always a way to change a data structure. The best it can do is the const qualifier, introduced earlier, which states to the compiler that a variable cannot be changed, i.e. assigned to, after it has been initialized.

For example:

```
const int myvar1=1:
```

is a declaration of a constant int and if you try to assign to it after the initial assignment in the declaration then your program will not compile. That is:

```
myvar=2;
```

will generate a compile-time error.

You can also use const with pointers, but unless you understand the use of the dereference operator in declarations things can be confusing.

For example, what is declared by:

```
const int *myvar2;
```

As before, you are declaring that *myvar2 is a constant int.

So myvar2 has to be a pointer to a constant int.

That is, the int is constant but the pointer isn't. The pointer can change and point to something else but the thing it points at can't be changed via the pointer. This means that:

```
const int myint1 = 1;
const int *myvar2;
myvar2 = &myint1;
```

is fine, but:

```
*myvar2 = 3;
```

isn't.

There is a subtlety here that is worth making clear. The pointer to a constant int can be set to point at a non-constant int. For example:

```
const int *myvar2;
int myvar3=2;
myvar2 = &myvar3;
myvar3=3;
```

is perfectly fine.

The fact that the pointer is to a constant `int` simply stops you from writing:

```
*myvar2=something;
```

All declaring a pointer to a constant type does is to stop you changing *something* via a pointer dereference - there may be other legal ways to change it.

It has to be admitted that different compilers react differently to any attempt to change a constant variable so you need to be careful.

Also, notice that you can write:

```
const int *myvar;
```

or:

```
int const *myvar;
```

and they mean the same thing - that `*myvar` is a constant integer.

However, if you move the dereferencing operator you get a very different result.

What does:

```
int *const myvar;
```

mean?

Here things are almost as logical and we read this as `myvar` is a constant and `*myvar` is an `int`. Notice that the pointer now cannot change, but the value of the `int` it points at can.

That is:

```
int myvar2 = 2;
int *const myvar1=&myvar2;
*myvar1 = 3;
```

is fine because the value 3 is stored in `myvar2`, which isn't constant, and `myvar1` points at `myvar2`, i.e. is constant throughout the program.

However:

```
myvar1 = &myvar3;
```

is not allowed.

Finally, if you can stand it, what does:

```
int myvar2 = 2;
const int  *const myvar1=&myvar2;
```

mean?

The answer is that this is a constant pointer to a constant integer. That is, `*myvar1` is a constant `int` and `myvar1` is a constant pointer.

You can't do:

```
myvar1=&myvar3;
```

as that would change the pointer; and you can't do:

```
*myvar1=48;
```

because that would change the int it is pointing at.

Once again, it is worth pointing out that you can still modify values if you use the variable directly rather than the pointer.

So while

```
*myvar1=48;
```

is illegal

```
myvar2=48;
```

is legal because myvar2 isn't a constant int.

In other words if you have a pointer then either the thing the pointer points at can be constant, the pointer can be constant, or both the pointer and the thing it points at can be constant.

So how would you make an immutable string?

You can create the const array using:

```
const char myString[]="Hello World";
myString[0]='h';
```

Note: you cannot use pointer notation because string literals are read only unless assigned to a char array and are stored in an area of memory that is generally set to read only.

The declaration says that myString is a const char and as a result the assignment to the first element will fail and the compiler will refuse to run the program.

This looks like a foolproof immutable string but all it takes is a cast to remove the effect of the const:

```
const char myString[]="Hello World";
char *myString2= (char*) myString;
myString2[0]='h';
printf("%s\n",myString);
```

Having changed the initial character in the string, this now prints hello World and the immutability has been overcome. With a suitable cast, C can modify any data.

Summary

- Declarations are always of the form
  type variable1, variable2, variable3...

- You can use the dereferencing operation in a declaration
  type variable1,*variable2 ...
  and *variable1* and **variable2* are *type* which means that *variable2* must be a pointer to *type*.

- Pointers and arrays are nearly, but not quite, the same thing. A simple array is a pointer constant allocated no storage, and a pointer is a variable pointer allocated storage.

- You can allocate and free memory using malloc and its associated functions.

- In C data is best regarded as a bit pattern. How that pattern is interpreted depends on its assigned type.

- You can also cast pointers and this changes how what they point at is interpreted.

- Type punning can be used to interpret the same bit pattern in different ways.

- In standard C type punning is undefined behavior and you should use unions as an alternative. Not every C programmer agrees with this point of view.

- You can use malloc and pointers to return arrays and other data structures from functions.

- Pointers to functions are also allowed and are useful in advanced contexts.

- You can also create pointers to pointers and so on. If a pointer is the same thing as a one-dimensional array, a pointer to a pointer can be thought of as a two-dimensional array and so on.

- You can use const to create immutable data – but this can be more complex than you might first think.

Chapter 11

Structs

The struct is perhaps the more sophisticated of the two "native" data structures that C has, the other being the array. It is true to say that with an array and a struct you can do just about anything, but to do anything safely you need to know exactly how structs work.

The Basic Struct

Structs have a slightly complicated syntax, but if you follow how they work it all makes sense. We have already met the array, which is a block of memory used to store a repeated type - i.e. an int array is a block of memory that stores one int after another. A struct is also a block of memory, but instead of being divided up into repeated copies of the same type it can be used for a fixed set of different types.

A struct is the programming equivalent of a record card with different types of data stored on it.

For example:

```
struct myStruct{
    char name[25];
    int  age;
};
```

defines a struct with a single string of 25 bytes followed by a single int of 2 or 4 bytes.

The different parts of a struct are sometimes called fields.

In the above example, struct is laid out in memory in a similar fashion to an array with name taking 25 bytes of the block of memory followed by the int. However, because different machines need to use memory aligned on particular byte boundaries, the size of the struct may not be what you expect. You have to allow for the possibility of padding bytes.

The struct declaration doesn't allocate memory for the struct and its doesn't create an instance of the struct that you can use. What it does is to create a struct type called myStruct, which can be used in a variable declaration just like int.

That is, to create an instance of `myStruct` you would use:

```
struct myStruct me;
```

where `me` is a variable that references a block of memory that has a 25-char array and a 2- or 4-byte int. Notice that the type is `struct myStruct` and not just `myStruct`. The name `myStruct` is usually called a tag. Notice that this is like the use of `enum` as part of the name in an enumeration.

If you want to create an instance along with the struct type declaration, you can:

```
struct myStruct{
    char name[25];
    int age;
} me;
```

Notice that this is just a standard declaration with `struct myStruct` being used as soon as it is declared. You can even drop the tag and use an anonymous struct to create an instance:

```
struct {
    char name[25];
    int age;
} me;
```

You can use this declaration to create multiple structs, for example:

```
struct {
    char name[25];
    int age;
} me, you, person;
```

but notice that you cannot reuse it at other points in your program as you haven't assigned a name to the type. Both of these idioms are common in C and can be confusing unless you understand that a struct is a type.

Once we have an instance of the new struct type, we can make use of it. You access the different components of a struct, not like an array, but using the dot name notation.

So, to set the age field, use:

```
me.age=19;
```

Setting the name field is just as easy, but being a string you need to use `strcpy` to set it to a string literal:

```
strcpy(me.name,"harry");
```

You can use the dot notation to print any of the fields of a struct:

```
printf("%d %s\n",me.age,me.name);
```

To initialize a struct you can simply provide the values for each field when an instance of the struct is created.

For example:

```
struct myStruct me={"harry",19};
```

the values are used to initialize the fields in the order that they are declared in the struct.

In C99 and later you can use a designated initializer:

```
struct myStruct me= {.age=19,.name="harry"};
```

and in this case the values are assigned to the named fields and they can be in any order.

At this point the main question to answer is why is a struct created in a two-stage process? Why define a struct type and then declare a variable of that type? The answer is that defining a struct can be quite complex, unlike say an array, and hence you don't want to repeat the exact form of the struct when you want to create an instance of it. For example, we can create another instance of the struct using:

```
struct myStruct person1;
```

and then use `person1` as before.

Another reason is that we often want to create an array of structs and this can be done in the usual way as `struct myStruct` is a type just like `int`.

For example:

```
struct myStruct people[25];
```

creates an array of 25 elements, each an instance of `myStruct`. You can access these using array and dot notation as you might expect:

```
people[3].age=34;
```

Put simply, structs are implemented as struct types to make it easier to declare multiple instances. Notice that struct types have the same scope as a variable. If you declare a struct type within a function, then it can only be used within that function. In addition a struct type cannot be used before it is declared.

Value Semantics

Defining a type for a struct is the first surprise, but if you have followed how the array works so well with reference semantics, you might be even more surprised to learn that structs use value semantics.

For example, if me and person are both instances of myStruct then:

```
person=me;
```

copies the fields of me into the fields of person.

To see this in action try:

```
struct myStruct me;
struct myStruct person;
me.age=19;
strcpy(me.name,"harry");
person=me;
person.age=21;
printf("%d %d\n",me.age,person.age);
```

You will see that me.age and person.age are two different fields in two different structs. A struct variable isn't a pointer to struct but a value like an int.

When you assign a struct to another struct of the same type the compiler generates code that copies the fields from the source struct to the destination struct.

It is important to realize at this early stage that struct assignment only performs a shallow copy. What this means is that the block of storage assigned to the struct is copied to the destination struct. This is usually all that is needed, but if the block contains a pointer to another block of memory then the pointer will be copied, but the block will not. That is, for structs that contain a pointer, the pointer is copied, but not what it points at. This is a shallow copy. A deep copy would make a copy of the pointer and what it pointed at.

You might be wondering what is happening with the name field – surely this is a pointer to a string, i.e. a char array and a shallow copy would fail to copy the data?

Does this mean that me and person share the same copy of the name string? If you try:

```
me.name[0]='X';
```

just before you print person you will discover that changing me.name doesn't change person.name. The reason is that the char array is declared within the struct and the 25 characters are actually stored in the struct. The constant pointer, i.e. the array variable me.name, references the 25 characters stored in the struct. When the me struct is assigned to the person struct the whole block of data including the 25 chars of the array are copied – hence they do not share the string.

Value semantics for structs doesn't seem to be better than reference semantics, which seem more natural.

Why are structs implemented in this way?

It is a matter of preference, but one reason why structs are value types is that they are often small and more like extensions of the basic integer types which use value semantics.

For example, a common use of a struct is to implement a coordinate type:

```
struct point{
    int x;
    int y;
}
```

This takes just twice the memory that a single int takes and it is convenient to treat it like an over-sized int type. This makes working with small structs easier:

```
struct point a = {0, 0};
struct point b;
b=a;
```

which assigns 0,0 to b. It is arguable that this is a more reasonable interpretation for this sort of struct than reference semantics, which would result in a and b pointing to the same data.

This said, many programmers are of the opinion that you should always avoid using value semantics with structs by using pointers to structs, see later.

Struct Parameters and Return

Value semantics also apply when you pass a struct to a function.

For example:

```
void addToAge(struct myStruct person) {
    person.age = person.age + 1;
}
```

In this case adding one to age has no effect on any struct in the main program and the function doesn't actually do anything useful. When you call it using:

```
addToAge(me);
```

it is as if the first thing that happens within the function is the equivalent of:

```
person = me;
```

and all of the fields of me are copied to person, i.e. value semantics.

187

The fact that structs use value semantics also means that you are safe to return a struct from a function. If the struct is local then it is destroyed when the function ends, but in this case it is not the struct that is returned, but the struct's value, which is copied into whatever variable in the main program the function is assigned to.

For example:

```
struct myStruct makePerson(char *name,int age){
    struct myStruct person;
    strncpy(person.name,name,25);
    person.age=age;
    return person;
}
```

This function creates and initializes a struct which it returns. It can be used in the obvious way:

```
struct myStruct me = makePerson("harry",19);
```

Notice that what happens is that the new struct me is set to harry, 19 by the return value of the person struct in the function.

The original struct is not returned, only its values are.

Finally, it is important to keep in mind that the copy involved in value semantics in a return is "shallow". The name field is stored within the struct and so it is copied along with the rest of the struct when the function returns. Any pointers to data outside of the struct would be copied, but not the data they point to.

Pointers to Structs

Using value semantics for structs makes reasonable sense if the struct is small and uses only a small amount of memory.

The reason arrays use reference semantics and structs use value semantics is that generally arrays are large whereas structs are small. Of course, there are times when structs are not small – mostly when one or more of the fields is an array.

Once structs get bigger then you should pass them by reference.

How big is it reasonable to pass a struct by value? The answer depends on the machine architecture you are working with but the important point is that the struct's values are usually passed on the stack so it is the stack size that matters, not the overall amount of memory available. This is particularly relevant if you pass a large struct to a function which then passes it to another function and so on. Each function call allocates the struct on the stack and so uses up increasing amounts of memory – this is particularly important in recursive calls.

In practice, things are more complex because the compiler could put the struct into a register and avoid the use of the stack, but this depends on the struct being very small and there being a register available for use.

In nearly all cases, it is faster to pass a struct by reference and this is generally considered to be best practice unless there is a really good reason not to.

How do you pass or return a struct by reference? Easy, you simply use a pointer to the struct. For example, the previous addToAge function that didn't work because person was passed by value, can be made to work by passing and using a pointer to the struct:

```
void addToAge(struct myStruct *person) {
    (*person).age = (*person).age + 1;
}
```

Notice that the parentheses are needed because the dereference operator has a lower precedence than the dot operator. Without the parentheses the expression would be equivalent to *(person.age), which wouldn't evaluate correctly.

Now you have to call addToAge using a pointer:

```
addToAge(&me);
```

and in this case the age field of me is changed by the function, which is what you would expect.

You can use a pointer to struct to return a struct but as in the case of an array the struct so returned cannot be a local variable. In other words you have to use malloc to allocate the memory on the heap.

For example, the makePerson function can be rewritten to create a struct on the heap:

```
struct myStruct* makePerson(char *name,int age){
    struct myStruct *person=
            (struct myStruct*)malloc(sizeof(struct myStruct));
    strncpy((*person).name,name,25);
    (*person).age=age;
    return person;
}
```

The cast isn't actually necessary but it makes clear what you intend. Notice that the function now returns a pointer to the struct and has to be called using:

```
struct myStruct *me = makePerson("harry",19);
```

The only downside of using a pointer to struct is the slightly cumbersome way you have to dereference the pointer within parentheses. To make this slightly easier, C introduced the -> notation which dereferences the pointer and accesses the field in one go, i.e. it's the equivalent of * and dot.

For example the makePerson function could be written:

```
struct myStruct* makePerson(char *name,int age){
    struct myStruct *person=
            (struct myStruct*)malloc(sizeof(struct myStruct));
    strncpy(person->name,name,25);
    person->age=age;
    return person;
}
```

and to print the fields you can use:

```
printf("%d %s\n", me->age, me->name);
```

It is generally considered good practice to use the arrow operator -> when you have a pointer to struct.

Notice that you can't simply use pointer arithmetic to access the fields of a struct. The reason is that adding one to a struct pointer treats it as if it was an array of structs and so it adds sizeof(struct) to the pointer. If you really want to access the fields you have to cast the pointer to the type of the first field and add one, then the next field and add one and so on until you reach the field of your choice. Even this isn't likely to work because of padding – see later.

In short don't try to access the fields of structs using pointer arithmetic, use the arrow -> notation.

Using typedef

Although it isn't really anything specifically associated with structs, typedef does tend to be used as a very common alternative way to define them.

A typedef is an alias for a type. For example:

```
typedef int myinttype;
```

defines myinttype to be an alias for int. Once defined you can use it as you would int. For example:

```
myinttype myVar;
```

declares myVar to be myinttype which is the same as int.

It is easy to misunderstand the way typedef works if you have only seen a simple example. It looks as if myinttype has been made equivalent to int, which is the overall effect, but a typedef is better understood as a modification of the usual declaration. Think of typedef as being a standard declaration where you are not declaring a variable, but an alias for a type. That is:

```
int myinttype;
```

declares the variable to be of type `int` whereas:

```
typedef int myinttype;
```

declares `myinttype` to be a type equivalent to `int`.

This becomes more easy to understand with more complex examples. For example:

```
typedef int *mypinttype;
```

defines `mypinttype` to be a pointer to `int`, but as a type not a variable. After this you can use it as:

```
mypinttype myPointer;
```

which declares `myPointer` as a pointer to `int`. For example:

```
typedef int myArray[20];
```

declares `myArray` to be an int array with 20 elements, but as a type. After this you can use it as:

```
myArray myRealArray;
```

and `myRealArray` is an int array with 20 elements.

You can use an alias anywhere you could use the original type and the compiler will not complain if you mix the use of the alias and the type.

Despite the fact that this doesn't add very much, this use of `typedef` can make your program more readable if you create type names that are more meaningful - `age_t`, say. On the other hand, a type alias hides the true type of a variable and as such might make your code harder to understand.

The real value in `typedef` is when it is used to create a shorter form of a longer type specification. In C there are three ways that such longer type definitions come into play – pointers, function types and structs. In the case of structs the whole point is to eliminate the need to include struct as part of the type name.

For example:

```
struct point {
     int x;
     int y;
};
typedef struct point point_t;
```

As a simple declaration, i.e. without `typedef`, this would make `point_t` an instance of `struct point`, but the `typedef` makes it an alias for the type. Now we can use `point_t` as an alias for `struct point`.

For example:

```
point_t myPoint={0,0};
```

This saves having to use `struct point` and you might think that this is a small advantage. However, the use of `typedef` to define an alias has become so common that many C programmers think it is the only way to create a struct! Combining the two declarations gives:

```
typedef struct point{
     int x;
     int y;
} point_t;
```

which looks a lot more like an integrated declaration of a struct rather than a combination of a `struct` declaration and a `typedef` – which is what it is. After this declaration you can use `struct point` or `point_t` to declare an instance of the struct.

You can also eliminate one of the identifiers by declaring an anonymous struct:

```
typedef struct{
     int x;
     int y;
} point;
```

and now it really does look as if this is the form of declaration for a struct.

Notice that you can use:

```
typedef struct point{
     int x;
     int y;
} point;
```

if you want as the `struct point` does not introduce the identifier `point` but the combined `struct point`.

The `typedef` idiom is very commonly used to create a `struct` but it is important to realize that it is a combination of `typedef` and a `struct` declaration.

Notice that:

```
struct point {
    int x;
    int y;
}myPoint;
```

creates an instance of point i.e. myPoint is a block of memory but:

```
typedef struct point {
    int x;
    int y;
}myPoint;
```

creates a type that has to be used in a declaration, i.e. myPoint is a type with no storage associated with it.

As well as structs, typedefs can make other complex declarations simpler. For example, consider defining a pointer to a particular function:

```
int *(pFunc)(int, int);
```

pFunc is a pointer to a function that takes two ints as parameters and returns an int. You can simplify this using:

```
typedef int *(pFunc_t)(int, int);
pFunc_t pFunc;
```

where now pFunc_t is a type specifying a pointer to a function that takes two ints and returns an int.

Nested Structs

You can define a struct that has a struct as a field, but you have to be careful how you do this. The reason is that you have to define a field instance not a type – what this means will become clear after an example.

The logically simplest way is to define the struct you want to nest as a type before you use it:

```
struct Address{
    char street[25];
    char zip[10];
};

struct Person{
    char name[25];
    struct Address add;
};
```

Notice the way that add is a field which is a struct in its own right. Internally all that happens in this case is that the compiler allocates a block of memory large enough to store the entire struct including the nested struct.

The only new feature is how to access the nested struct. You simply use the dot notation more than once:

```
struct Person me;
strcpy(me.name,"Harry");
strcpy(me.add.street,"mystreet");
```

The same applies if you are using pointers. Simply use the number of dots or arrows to get to the inner nested structs. Notice that once you have dereferenced a pointer you can use the dot notation for the nested struct.

For example, if p_me is a pointer to Person then to access street you would use:

```
p_me -> add.street
```

We can create a definition of the nested struct directly:

```
struct Person {
    char name[25];
    struct Address {
        char street[25];
        char zip[10];
    }add;
};
```

Notice that again we need to create an instance of the nested struct. You can also eliminate the need to name the nested struct:

```
struct Person {
    char name[25];
    struct {
        char street[25];
        char zip[10];
    }add;
};
```

Having said all of this, it is worth pointing out that most compilers will allow an extension to the C standard and will allow an anonymous struct to be used without creating a field.

For example:

```
struct Person {
    char name[25];
    struct {
        char street[25];
        char zip[10];
    };
};
```

will create a Person struct that has fields .street and .zip, i.e. the fields of the nested struct are directly accessible.

Padding

As mentioned at the start of the chapter, a `struct` allocates memory that is large enough to contain all of the fields, but in many cases it will allocate more memory than you might predict. The reason for this is the need for memory accesses to be aligned to word boundaries. For example in a 32-bit machine the address of a 32-bit int would have to be a multiple of four because the memory is divided into 4-byte words accessible in a single read/write. Some machines demand that memory accesses are aligned, others allow it but warn that it is slower. If alignment is optional but slower, some compilers have an option that lets you decide if you want to pack the `struct` for minimum space or include padding to ensure that fields are aligned correctly for speed. What all this means is that you cannot simply assume that a `struct` takes the amount of space suggested by how much space its fields take.

For a 64-bit machine using a 64-bit word then a `struct` will take at least eight bytes.

For example:

```
struct test {
    int i;
    char c;
}test;
printf("%d \n", sizeof (int));
printf("%d \n", sizeof (char));
printf("%d \n", sizeof (struct test));
```

will print 4, 1 and 8 on a 64-bit Intel processor based machine. So although the `struct` should have taken just five bytes it actually takes eight to pad it out to a full 64 bit word.

Notice that the padding is added at the end or in between fields. The C standard ensures that no padding is added to the start of a `struct` and this means you can rely on the fact that the address of the struct is the address of the first field.

If you add:

```
printf("%d \n",&test);
printf("%d \n",&test.i);
printf("%d \n",&test.c);
```

to the end of the previous example you will see that &test and &test.i are at the same address and &test.c is likely to be `sizeof(int)` further on. This means that the padding is at the end of the `struct`.

It isn't always the case that the padding is added at the end.

For example, swapping the order of char and int:

```
struct test {
    char c;
    int i;
} test;
```

give you a strut with the same size but the addresses are now such that test.c is at the start of the struct but test.i is likely to be four bytes from the start of the struct. That is, there are three bytes of padding between test.c and test.i. It is as if the struct was declared as:

```
struct test {
    char c;
    char padding[3];
    int i;
} test;
```

Similar things happen with short ints and other sizes of integer types, their addresses generally have to be on a multiple of their size e.g int address is divisible by four, long by eight and short by two.

Notice that what padding actually occurs depends on the machine architecture and the compiler options.

If you want to pack a struct to take the smallest amount of memory then a rule of thumb is to allocate fields in the order of size starting with the largest.

In general optimizing the packing of a struct isn't necessary unless you are using a great many of them – then it can be essential. Notice that such optimizations are always machine dependent.

Union

The union is a special type of struct and not one you are likely to use on a regular basis. In many cases you can avoid its use by simply casting to the type you require as explained in the previous chapter, but using a union is the only valid C standard way of doing the job.

A union is declared in the same way as a struct but memory is only allocated for the largest of the union fields. That is, all of the fields of a union share the same memory. This sounds like a crazy thing to do until you notice that it gives you a way of working with the same bit pattern with different interpretations.

That is, the union allows you to do well-defined type punning in C (but not in C++).

For example:

```
union {
    int a;
    float b;
}test;

test.b=3.14;
printf("%d\n",test.a);
```

The union declares a four byte int and an eight byte float both sharing the same memory locations. The union is eight bytes in total and both the int and the float start at the beginning of the memory allocated – there is no padding at the start of a struct or a union. When we refer to test.a or test.b we are accessing the same area of memory and so test.a accesses the first four bytes of the float which we print in the last line.

This probably isn't of much use as an integer derived from the first four bytes of a float isn't easy to interpret but it shows the general principle. If you want the first four bytes of a float interpreted as an int then a union is one way to do it.

You don't need a union to do the job as a cast can be used to interpret any type as the bit pattern of another type. In this case, however, the cast required is complex and not at all obvious:

```
float pi=3.14;
printf("%d\n",*(int *)&pi);
```

This works by taking the address of the float, i.e. &pi, casting this to a pointer to int and finally dereferencing it to get the value stored in the first four bytes. Of course under strict aliasing rules this type cast is undefined behavior.

If you want to avoid undefined behavior then you should use a union to perform the equivalent of type punning.

For a more realistic example consider the way most graphics hardware stores a ARGB – Alpha, Red, Green and Blue value in an unsigned 32 bit int. If you want to access each of these bytes and also treat all four bytes as a single value then the best way is to define a union:

```
union Pixel{
    struct {unsigned char b,g,r,a;};
    uint32_t value;
};
```

The only complication is that the order has to be change to allow for way x86 stores multiple bytes in a 32 bit word - see Chapter 12 Endianism.

Now you can declare a pixel and use it as follows:

```
union Pixel pixel;
pixel.r=1;
pixel.g=255;
pixel.b=128;
pixel.a=255;
printf("%d\n",pixel.value);
```

If you can't use an anonymous struct you can substitute a char array say.

A union can always be used in place of type punning but it often requires a little more pre-planning. For example, we can write the example given in Chapter 10 concerning reading in four bytes and treating these as a single int as:

```
union dualbuffer{
   char Cbuffer[100];
   int  Ibuffer[25];
}buffer;

buffer.Cbuffer[0]=1;
buffer.Cbuffer[1]=2;
buffer.Cbuffer[2]=3;
buffer.Cbuffer[3]=4;
printf("%d \n",buffer.Ibuffer[0]);
```

You can see that the union aliases the two arrays – a byte array and an int array.

The point is that if you construct a suitable union which aliases the same types that you would alias using type punning then you never have to use type punning. Indeed recently some programmers refer to this use of unions as type punning.

Although the main use of unions in low-level C programming is to perform type punning, this is not what more general programmers tend to think a union is for. Many programmers and especially those more familiar with higher level languages see unions as ways of saving storage or creating flexible data structures often called variants or tagged unions.

For example, suppose you have a name record which sometimes has a telephone number as a string and sometimes as an integer. You could store this as:

```
struct {
        int type;
        union {
            char numstring[10];
            int numint;
        } phone;
} person;
```

Notice that the Phone fields are a union of char[10] and int. The type field is the tag indicating which type is in use.

For example:

```
person.type=1;
strcpy(person.phone.numstring,"1234");
person.type=0;
person.phone.numint=1234;
```

When trying to access the field you would test the type field first.

In this example, it is obvious that you should parse the telephone field into a standard format but there are situations where this doesn't make sense.

If the compiler supports anonymous unions we can get rid of the phone field which seems unnecessary:

```
struct {
        int type;

        union {
            char numstring[10];
            int numint;
        };
} person;
```

Now we can write:

```
person.type = 1;
strcpy(person.numstring, "1234");
person.type = 0;
person.numint = 1234;
```

GCC supports this use of an anonymous union but NetBean's parser flags that it cannot find person.numstring or person.numint – even though the program works.

Bit Fields

Structs have one final feature – bit fields. A bit field is a way of breaking down the storage into even smaller units than bytes. You can define a bit field within a struct by following the field definition by a colon and the number of bits.

For example:

```
struct Bits{
    int bit1:1;
    int bit2:1;
};
```

creates an int, say four bytes, but only the first two bits are used. This is somewhat like a union, but in this case the bit fields share the int.

For example:

```
struct Bits bits;
bits.bit1=1;
bits.bit2=1;
printf("%d\n",bits);
```

If we make a small change to the `struct` then you can see that you can work with more than just single bits:

```
struct Bits{
    int byte:8;
    int bit1:1;
    int bit2:1;
}bits;
```

This divides up the int so that the first eight bits are called `byte`, followed by two single-bit fields. Now we can write:

```
bits.bit1=1;
bits.bit2=1;
bits.byte=255;
printf("%d\n",bits);
printf("%d\n",bits.byte);
```

you will discover that `bits` is `1023` and `bits.byte` is -1.

As the `int` being shared is a `signed int` then so are all of the fields including the single-bit fields:

```
printf("%d\n",bits.bit1);
```

prints -1.

The standards are unclear on whether a bit field `int` is to be interpreted as signed or unsigned.

You can change the interpretation of a single field using:

```
struct Bits{
    unsigned int byte:8;
    int bit1:1;
    int bit2:1;
}bits;
```

`bits.byte` now prints 255 but `bits.bit1` still prints -1.

You can often use other types, not just `int`, but this goes beyond standard C. If you mix types then usually the largest type is used.

For example:

```
struct Bits{
    unsigned char byte:8;
    char bit1:1;
    char bit2:1;
}bits;
```

usually allocates a `char` for the first eight bits and another `char` for the next two bits giving an overall size of two bytes for the struct.

It is usually better to keep all of the bit fields the same type within a struct.

In general no padding is used in a bit field but if you allocate more bits than an int can represent, a second `int` is used. If you want to force a new allocation so that a bit field is aligned to an address boundary you can include an unnamed bit field of size zero.

For example:

```
struct Bits{
    unsigned int byte:8;
    int :0;
    int bit1:1;
    int bit2:1;
}bits;
```

This allocates two `ints` with `bits.byte` occupying the first eight bits of the first int and `bits.bit1` and `bits.bit2` at the start of the second byte.

You can form expressions with bit fields and any result will not overflow into an adjacent bit field.

For example:

```
bits.byte=255;
bits.byte++;
```

results in `bits.byte` overflowing and it is set to zero, but `bits.bit1` isn't changed.

Notice that you cannot have a pointer to a bit field, but you can have a pointer to the `struct` that has bit fields. This is often useful when you want to map a bit field to a hardware port or register.

For example, suppose there is a hardware register at `0x01000` and its first four bits control the brightness of LED1 and the next four control LED2. You could interface with it using a bit field:

```
struct Port{
    int led1:4;
    int led2:4;
}
Port *port=(port*) 0x01000;
```

Now we have a pointer of type `Port` to the location, we can set LED1 and LED2 using statements like:

```
*port.led1=3;
*port.led2=15;
```

This is a very attractive approach in that it is easy to read, but it has a big disadvantage in that different compilers implement bit fields in different ways. If you are working with hardware in this way, the chances are that you will be using a fixed compiler and portability isn't an issue. On the other hand, if the layout of bit fields does change for any reason your program will stop working.

For these reasons many programmers recommend avoiding the use of bit fields and implementing the bit operations manually, which is the subject of the Chapter 12.

Summary

- A struct is a block of memory used to store a set sequence of data types - its fields. It corresponds to the idea of a record.

- A struct is declared as a type which can be used to create as many instances of the type as required.

- The fields of a struct are accessed using the dot notation, struct.field, or if you are using a pointer to a struct then you can use the arrow notation, pstruct->field.

- Structs are assigned using value semantics. That is a copy is created on assignment, or when used as a parameter or returned via a function. The copy is shallow – i.e. any pointers are copied but not memory external to the struct they may point at.

- A typedef statement can be used to create an alias for a type. It is often used in conjunction with a struct declaration and this can be confusing for the beginner.

- Structs can be nested. The nested struct has memory allocated for it within the containing struct.

- A complication of using structs is padding. Extra bytes often have to be added to a struct to make its fields align with word boundaries.

- A union is a special type of struct that only allocates memory for the largest of its fields. All other fields share the same memory. A union can be used to alias types, that is the same block of memory is treated as different types. This is the only standard based way of achieving type punning.

- A struct field can be allocated at the bit level. This sounds attractive but implementation differences make it worth avoiding.

Chapter 12

Bit Manipulation

Bit manipulation is almost dead in high-level languages and it isn't as common in C as it once was. If you are writing low-level programs that interact in any way with the hardware, however, then bit manipulation will still be an essential part of what you do and, to get things right and to make sure you are doing things in sensible ways, you need to master the technique. The good news is that it isn't difficult once you start to think about the contents of memory as a bit pattern that has many interpretations.

The Bitwise Operators

C has a number of operators designed to allow you to perform bit manipulation. There are four bitwise operators:

AND	&
OR	|
XOR (exclusive or)	^
NOT	~

As you would expect the NOT operator has the highest priority.

Notice that there are also corresponding Boolean operators &&, || and ! which only work with Boolean values – with zero as false and anything non-zero as true - and not with bit patterns.

The bitwise operators work with integer types. For example:

```
int a = 0xF0;
int b = 0xFF;
int c = ~a & b;
printf("%X\n",c)
```

This first works out the bitwise NOT of a, i.e. 0F. This is then bitwise ANDed with b, i.e. 0F & FF which is F. The %X format specifier prints the value in hex. You can use %x for lower case and %d for decimal.

Signed v Unsigned

Now we come to a subtle and troublesome point. Bitwise operators are only uniquely defined for unsigned values. The reason is that unsigned values have an unambiguous representation in binary and hence the operations are well-defined in terms of the values the bit patterns represent.

That is:

```
unsigned int value=5;
```

is always `0101` and hence:

```
value | 0x2
```

is not only always `0111`, but also always represents +7.

The same is not true for signed values simply because the way in which negative numbers are represented isn't fixed. The most common representation is two's complement, but this is not part of the standard and so logical operations on unsigned numbers are implementation-dependent. Notice that this does not mean logical operations on signed values are undefined behavior – if this was the case most C programs would stop working properly. In addition "implementation-dependent" has one fairly consistent meaning:

> *take the bit pattern that represents the value and perform the specified logical operation as if everything involved was an unsigned value.*

This is the only sane way to deal with the problem and it is exactly what you would expect. So, where the bit pattern isn't defined, as in:

```
signed int value=-5;
```

if the machine uses two's complement representation, see Chapter 5, then the bit pattern is:

```
11111111111111111111111111111011
```

and

```
value | 0x4
```

changes the third bit to 1 i.e. -1 in two's complement.

As long as you assume a representation for the signed value then the logical operation is usually well defined as the bitwise application of the operator on the bit patterns. It is the representation that is implementation-dependent and not the operation.

Masks

So what do you use the bitwise logical operators for?

In many cases you have the problem of setting or clearing particular bits in a value. The value is usually stored in a variable that is usually regarded as a status variable or flag.

You can set and unset bits in a flag using another value, usually called a mask, that defines the bits to be changed.

For example if you only want to change the first (least significant) bit then the mask would be 0x01.

If you wanted to change the first and second bits the mask would be 0x03 and so on.

If you find working out the correct hexadecimal value needed for any particular mask difficult then you could use the strtol function with a radix of two. For example:

```
char *prt;
int a = strtol("01",&prt,2);
```

sets a to 0x01 and:

```
int a = strtol("11",&prt,2);
```

sets a to 0x03 and so on.

To create a mask just write down a string of zeros and ones with ones in the positions you want to change and use strtol to convert to a mask value.

Now that you have a mask what do you do with it?

Suppose the variable mask contains a value that in binary has a one at each bit location you want to change. Then:

```
flag | mask;
```

returns a bit pattern with the same bits set to one as in the mask. Notice that the bits that the mask doesn't specify, i.e. are zero in the mask, are left at their original values.

For example:

```
char *prt;
int mask = strtol("11",&prt,2);
int flag = 0xFFF0;
int result = flag | mask;
printf("%X\n",result);
```

sets result to 0xFFF3, i.e. it sets the first (least significant) two bits.

If you use:

```
flag & ~mask;
```

then the bits specified in the mask are set to zero - or are unset if you prefer. Notice that you have to apply a NOT operator to the mask.

For example:

```
char *prt;
int mask = strtol("11",&prt,2);
int flag = 0xFFFF;
int result = flag & ~mask;
printf("%X\n",result);
```

sets result to 0xFFFC, i.e. it unsets the first two bits.

As well as setting and unsetting particular bits, you might also want to "flip" the specified bits, i.e. negate them so that if the bit was a one it is changed to a zero and vice versa. You can do this using the exclusive or (XOR) operator:

```
flag ^ mask
```

flips the bits specified by the mask.

For example:

```
char *prt;
int mask = strtol("11",&prt,2);
int flag = 0xFFFF;
int result = flag ^ mask;
printf("%X\n",result);
```

sets result to 0xFFFC because it changes the lower two bits from ones to zeros. Again bits not specified by mask are unaffected.

Of course, in each case you don't have to use a variable to specify the mask you could just use a numeric literal.

For example instead of:

```
int flag = 0xFFFF;
int result = flag ^ mask;
```

you can write:

```
int result = flag ^ 0xFFFF;
```

Also, if you want to update the flag rather than derive a new result, you can use:

```
&=
|=
```

and:

```
^=
```

to perform the update directly.

For example, instead of:

```
int flag = flag ^ 0xFFFF;
```

you can use:

```
int flag ^=  0xFFFF;
```

To summarize:

- create a mask that has 1 at the position of each bit you want to change.
- OR the mask with the flag to set just those bits.
- AND the NOT of the mask to unset just those bits.
- XOR the mask to flip just those bits.

Bits in the mask that are 0 are unaffected by any of the operations.

Using Masks

What sorts of things do you use masking operations for?

Often a low-level API will require that particular bits in a status word are set or unset to make it operate in a particular way. Similarly, hardware registers are generally organized into groups of bits that you have to change to control the device.

A very common application is to extract the RGB color information from a single int representing the color of a pixel. For example:

```
int RGBcolor=0x010203;
int B=RGBcolor & 0x0000FF;
int G=RGBcolor & 0x00FF00;
int R=RGBcolor & 0xFF0000;
```

takes an RGB value and splits it up into its components using appropriate masks. The result is that you end up with 0x010000 stored in R, 0x000200 in G and 0x000003 in B. Notice that the value of B is correct, but R and G are incorrect - the bits need shifting to the right. This brings us to the use of the shift operators.

Shifting Values

As well as the basic logical operators, C also provides two shift operators which move the pattern of bits to the left or the right.

The << operator shifts the pattern of bits to the left shifting in zero into the low-order. So for example:

```
int data=0x0F;
int result=data << 4;
```

shifts the bit pattern in data four places to the left and so result contains 0xF0.

Similarly the >> operator shifts to the right, but there is a small complication concerning what is shifted into the new bit positions. What happens depends on whether the value being shifted is signed or unsigned.

For an unsigned value 0 is shifted into the highest order bit.

For a signed value the same bit is shifted in as the one moved out. That is, if the highest order bit was a 1 then a 1 is shifted into the vacant position and it if was a 0 a 0 is shifted in.

You can see that in the signed case the motivation with a right shift is to maintain the sign. That is, a shift keeps a positive number positive and a negative number negative. This sort of shift is usually called an arithmetic shift as distinct from a logical shift that always shifts a 0 in.

Notice that a left shift always shifts a 0 in, but this can change the sign of the value as a new bit becomes the sign bit. For example:

```
int data=0x0F;
int result=data >>3;
```

shifts the bit pattern in data three places to the right and so result contains 1 since 1111 shifted three places right is 0001.

Notice that, for integers, shifting one place to the left is the same as multiplying the value by two and shifting one place to the right is the same as integer division by two but only for positive values. For example:

```
int data=1;
int result=data <<1;
```

stores 2 in result and:

```
int data=8;
int result=data >>1;
```

stores 4 in result.

Things are slightly more complicated for negative values. If you try

```
int data=7;
int result=data >>1;
```

then result is 3 which is what you would get with integer division i.e. 3.5 is truncated or rounded down to 3. However if you try:

```
int data=-7;
int result=data >>1;
```

you will find that result is -4. This is not what you would get with integer division which would give -3 after truncation. Right shift divides by 2 but with rounding towards the next smallest negative integer. This is a subtle point that often causes errors.

The reason for this behavior is the way the sign bit is extended For example:

```
int data=-1;
int result=data >>1;
```

stores -1 in result. The reason is that the initial bit pattern is all ones, i.e. 32 bits all set to one, and so shifting one place to the right shifts in another 1 as the high bit. That is, -1 is the same as 0xFFFFFFFF and the sign bit is 1 so a shift right moves a one into the high-order bit giving -1 again.

Compare this to:

```
unsigned int data=-1;
int result=data >>1;
```

In this case a zero is shifted into the high bit and the value stored in result gives zero followed by 31 ones, which is a positive value equal to 2147483647.

Notice that the -1 is stored in data as 0xFFFFFFFF but this is interpreted as a positive value when stored in an unsigned int. The result of the shift is 0x7FFFFFFF which is a positive number when assigned to a signed int.

What this means is that you can use either right and left shifts or multiplication and division by two to do almost the same job with a little care over negative values. Shifts are much faster than multiplication and division because the hardware generally supports a direct shift operation in a register.

If you want a logical right shift on a signed value then the simplest way of implementing it is to use a cast:

```
int data=-1;
int result=(unsigned) data >>1;
```

Also notice that you can write <<= and >>= to shift the value of a variable "in place". For example:

```
int data=-1;
data<<= 1
```

shifts the bit pattern in data one place to the left and stores the result in data, i.e. it shifts data one place to the left.

Typically shifts can be useful when you are normalizing values after having extracted bits using a mask. For example consider the problem of separating out the RGB values given earlier:

```
int RGBcolor=0x010203;
int B=RGBcolor & 0x0000FF;
int G=RGBcolor & 0x00FF00;
int R=RGBcolor & 0xFF0000;
G>>=8;
R=(unsigned)R>>16;
int data=-1;
data<<= 1;
```

Now R is 1, G is 2 and B is 3, as required. Notice that we can shift G without worrying about the sign bit because it has to be 0. When we shift R then we have to use a logical shift to stop it being interpreted as a negative value.

Of course, you can combine the operations into a single expression:

```
int RGBcolor=0x010203;
int B=RGBcolor & 0x0000FF;
int G=(RGBcolor & 0x00FF00)>>8;
int R=((unsigned)RGBcolor & 0xFF0000) >>16;
```

Because the shift operator has a higher priority than logical &, the brackets are needed.

Rotate

There is another form of shift – the left or right rotate – and while most processors have an instruction that will perform this type of shift in a single operation, for reasons of history C doesn't have a rotate operator.

A right rotate shifts all of the bits to the right and uses the least significant bit that is shifted out as the new most significant. That is, the low-order bit is shifted into the high-order bit. You can see that this is rotation of the bits.

Similarly a left rotate shifts all of the bits left and moves the high-order bit to become the new low-order bit. Again you can see that this rotates the bits in the other direction. Rotations don't correspond to simple multiplication or division and they aren't useful in the same way as left and right shifts are in isolating bits. What they are used for is in cryptography and signal processing.

C may not have a rotate operator. but it is easy to implement a rotate using left and right rotates and logical operators.

For example a right rotate is:

```
unsigned int data=0xF;
data= data>>1 | data<<31;
```

The idea is easy enough to understand. First we perform a right logical shift which leaves the most significant bit zeroed. Next we perform a left logical shift 31 times to move the lowest significant bit to become the highest significant bit. The two are ORed together to give the result 0x80000007.

You can see the general principle. If you want a right rotate of n bits of a 32-bit int then use:

```
data= data>>n | data<<32-n;
```

Similarly, if you want a left rotate of n bits of a 32-bit value then use:

```
data= data<<n | data>>32-n;
```

Notice that n cannot be negative or equal to 32, which would trigger undefined behavior. Also notice that data has to be unsigned so as to use logical shifts.

It is said that most compilers will detect the above idioms and convert the instructions into a machine code rotate instruction if possible. GCC does this optimization, but only if you make sure that the rotation is positive. That is:

```
unsigned int data=0x0F;
data= data>> (unsigned) 1 | data<< (unsigned)31;
```

compiles to:

```
ror  %eax
```

where ror is a rotate right instruction. If you leave off the unsigned qualifiers the line compiles to the equivalent right shift and left shift ORed together.

It would be better if C had a rotate operator.

Testing a Bit

One common requirement is to test if a particular bit is set or unset. Actually it is just as easy to test for any number of bits set or unset because the job is done using a mask. As before, if you create a mask with bits set corresponding to the bits you want to test, then:

```
value & mask
```

returns 0 if and only if all of the bits the mask specifies are 0.

Similarly:

```
~ value & mask
```

returns 0 if and only if all of the bits the mask specifies are 1.

Usually you only want to test for a single bit. For example:

```
int value=0x1F;
int mask=0x10;
int result=~value & mask;
```

tests the fifth bit in value which is 1 and so result is 0.

213

If you test for the fifth bit to be a zero using:

```
int value=0x1F;
int mask=0x10;
int result=value & mask;
```

then the result is non-zero, 16 to be precise.

If you want to convert the test results to Boolean values you can use the logical operator !.

For example:

```
!(~value & mask)
```

is true if and only if all of the bits in value specified by mask are 1 and false otherwise.

Similarly:

```
!(value & mask)
```

is true if and only if all of the bits in the value specified by mask are 0 and false otherwise.

Endianism

A problem that often arises in bit manipulation is endianism. When you design a computer there is a choice to be made. If parts of a word, say each byte, has a separate address do you store the low-order bits at low addresses, little endian, or at high addresses, big endian?

For example, consider a 2-byte int and alias it to a 2-byte array.

```
union endian{
    short unsigned int myint;
    unsigned char mychar[2];
}test;
test.myint=0x00FF;
printf("%x \n",test.mychar[0]);
printf("%x \n",test.mychar[1]);
```

The union aliases myint and mychar. We then set myint so that all its low-order first 8 bits are 1. If the machine is little endian, as in the case of x86 and ARM, then the low-order bits are stored in mychar[0]. If the machine is big endian, e.g. Atmel AVR32, the low-order bits are stored in mychar[1].

For example, creating a union to access the separate ARGB – Alpha, Red, Green and Blue values in an unsigned 32 bit int given in Chapter 10 is an example of something that changes according to endianism. As A is the high order byte and B the low order you might expect the union to be:

```
union Pixel{
    struct {unsigned char a,r,g,b;};
    uint32_t value;
};
```

and this works for big endian systems as b the least significant byte has the highest address in the union.

However the x86 and ARM are little endian. So the ARGB bytes are stored in the opposite order with a at the lowest address in the union:

```
union Pixel{
    struct {unsigned char b,g,r,a;};
    uint32_t value;
};
```

It is not only machine architecture that determines endianism. Data is transmitted in big endian format over most Internet protocols – IPv4, IPv6, UDP, TCP etc. What this means is that if you are using a machine with little endian format you transmit mychar[1] before mychar[0] to send a 16-bit integer when using almost any Internet protocol. That is it is the order that data is sent and received rather than addressing that is variable.

Notice that some machines support both big and little endian and you can select which is used. It is also possible for different data formats, e.g. integer and floating point, to use different orders. You will also find issues of which byte goes first when you use memory-mapped devices. In this case a careful reading of the data sheet usually solves the problem. If you are getting strange results and are sending data processed in bytes then you need to consider endianism.

Some Examples

The very basic bit manipulation operations are needed almost as soon as you start to work with the hardware. Usually the status and data associated with a device are packed into bytes or words as bit fields and you need to access them using masks. An alternative is to use a struct and define bit fields that give you access to the hardware. This works, but you cannot rely on its portability and the compiler might change how it handles bit fields. In general, it is safer to use masks and this is what the compiler uses to implement bit fields.

There are also lots of cases where bit manipulation enters into algorithms that have very little to do with accessing the hardware. It can take a leap of imagination to even notice that there is an alternative way to do the job.

Options

A very simple example of bit manipulation is the use of an `enum` to implement a flexible system of options. For example, suppose you wanted to allow the user to specify options in a graphics function call – `FILL`, `EDGE` and `ROUND`. It doesn't matter what these represent, the important part is that they are not mutually exclusive and the user can select any subset.

The standard way of doing this job is to define a set of bit masks as an `enum`:

```
enum gOptions {FILL=0x01,EDGE=0x02,ROUND=0x04}
```

Notice that the values are powers of two. If you pass any of these options to the function then all it has to do is test for that particular bit being set.

For example, after:

```
gFunction(FILL);
```

the mask has bit `0` set. If you want multiple options then simply OR them together:

```
gFunction(FILL | ROUND)
```

gives a result that has bit 0 and bit 2 set.

The function can use the same `enum` to test for bits set:

```
if(option & ROUND)
```

is only true if bit 2 is set in `option`.

You will find this sort of scheme implemented in many supplied functions.

Overflow Free Average

Consider finding the average of two integers. The simple straightforward way of doing the job is:

```
int average=(a+b)/2;
```

This has one problem – `a+b` can overflow even if the answer is representable in the number of bits available. At first it looks as if nothing can be done but if a result can be represented then there is usually a bit-manipulation way of computing it without the threat of overflow.

In this case we need to notice that addition is a simple logical operation. If you add the two values, `a` and `b` together then the sum bits are:

```
a ^ b
```

and the carry bits are:

```
a & b
```

this is how a half adder is implemented.

For example:

```
a        1 0 1
b        0 1 1
sum      1 1 0
carry  0 0 1
```

To get the final result you have to add the carry bits to the next highest bit of the result. So a left shift and an addition:

```
1 1 0 +   (0 0 1  <<1)
```

gives 1 0 0 0

That is:

a+b= (a^b)+(a&b)<<1

and so:

(a+b)/2=(a^b)>>1 + (a&b)

which can be computed with no risk of overflow.

Computing a Checksum

A CRC – Cyclic Redundancy Checksum – is a common implementation requirement. Many devices send data protected by a CRC, which is sent as the last few bytes. The idea is that you read in the data, compute the CRC and compare it to the CRC that has been sent with the data. If they are the same then you can be relatively secure in the belief that the data has been received without an error. For example, the simplest CRC is the sum of all the bits. If the computed sum of bits doesn't match the transmitted sum of bits you know a bit has gone missing. However, you don't know there is an error if two or more bits have simply swapped their positions.

Typically a CRC is defined by specifying a polynomial. The idea is that each term in the polynomial corresponds to a bit position in a shift register.

For example the polynomial used by 1-wire devices is:

$X^8 + X^5 + X^4 + 1$

There is a lot of theory about how CRCs work and their relationship to polynomial division and shift registers. It is a really interesting and useful theory, but all you really need to know is that the polynomial defines the structure of a shift register with feedback:

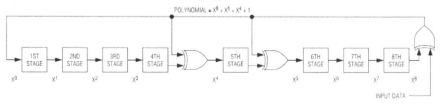

217

The first question to answer is what is the connection between binary values and polynomials?

The answer is that you can treat a binary number as the coefficients of a polynomial, for example 101 is $1*X^2+0*X+1$. Each bit position corresponds to a power of X. Using this notation creates a very simple relationship between multiplying by X and a left shift. For example:

```
(1*X² + 0*X+ 1)*X = 1*X³ + 0*X² + 1X + 0
```

corresponds to:

```
101 <<1 == 1010
```

You can see that this extends to multiplying one polynomial by another and even polynomial division, all accomplished by shifting and XORing.

The CRC is the remainder when you divide the polynomial that represents the data by the generator polynomial. The computation of the remainder is what the shift register does.

The fact that the division can be implemented so simply in hardware is what makes this sort of CRC computation so common. All the hardware has to do is zero the shift register and feed the data into it. When all the data has been shifted in, what is left in the shift register is the CRC, i.e. the remainder.

To check the data you have received all you have to do is run it through the shift register again and compare the computed CRC with the one received. A better trick is also to run the received CRC though the shift register. If there have been no errors this will result in 0.

We now know everything we need to if we want to implement this CRC. All we have to do is implement the shift register in software. From the diagram, what we have to do is take each bit of the input data and XOR it with the least significant bit of the current shift register. If the input bit is 0 then the XORs in the shift register don't have any effect and the CRC just has to be moved one bit to the right. If the input bit is 1, you have to XOR bits at positions 3 and 4 with 1 and we have to put a 1 in at position 7 to simulate shifting a 1 into the register, i.e. XOR the shift register with 10001100 or 0x8C.

So the algorithm for a single byte contained in databyte is:

```
for (int j = 0; j < 8; j++) {
    temp = (crc ^ databyte) & 0x01;
    crc >>= 1;
    if (temp){
            crc ^= 0x8C;
            databyte>>= 1;
            }
}
```

First we XOR the data with the current CRC and extract the low-order bit into temp. Then we right shift the CRC by one place. If the low-order result, stored in temp was a 1, you have to XOR the CRC with 0x8C to simulate the XORs in the shift register and shift in a 1 at the most significant bit. Then shift the data one place right and repeat for the next data bit.

Now all we have to do is use this to process each databyte through the CRC and use the final value in crc either to send along with the data as a check, or to compare to the received CRC value to see if there is an error.

There are many optimizations that you can apply to make computing a CRC work faster and you may be able to use a library version. However, there are so many different CRC polynomials that you might have to implement your own and this is a good starting point.

Summary

- There are four bitwise logical operators &, |, ^ and ~. These should not be confused with the logical operators &&, || and !.

- The bitwise logical operators behave differently on signed and unsigned types.

- A mask is a way of controlling which bits a bitwise operation affects.

- There are two shift operators: the << arithmetic or logical shift left and >> an arithmetic shift right.

- Arithmetic shift left corresponds to multiplying an integer type by 2 and an arithmetic shift right divides by 2.

- Arithmetic shift right isn't exactly the same as integer division by 2 for negative values as it rounds towards negative infinity.

- There is no rotate operator in C, but you can construct one.

- Masks can also be used to test the state of a bit or group of bits.

- There is no standard for the order in which parts of a multi-byte value are stored. Little endian stores the low-order bits first and big endian stores the high-order bits first.

Chapter 13

Files

File handing is a difficult area because providing files and file access is the responsibility of the operating system and so cannot be really platform-independent. However, C does provide some standard file handling functions in the standard library and these are where you start, no matter what the machine or operating system.

The whole subject of file handling and file I/O is a very big one and there are many functions that are involved in format conversion and so on that we haven't the space to cover. Once you have seen the basic and most commonly used functions, then the remainder are fairly easy to understand.

There is also a second set of file handling commands that are found on Linux and Unix systems – the file descriptor, which is covered in *Applying C For The IoT With Linux*.

The File Idea

If you are working with Unix or Linux there is an important principle concerning files that it is worth knowing – everything is a file. If you consider a file to be a stream of bytes, either on their way into the machine or on their way out of the machine, you can see that this idea covers many situations. You can consider a file stored on disk to be a Linux file, but you can also regard the stream of bytes generated by typing on a keyboard to be a file. As will become clear, even low-level sensors and devices can often be regarded as files. For this reason alone it is worth mastering C files at an early stage.

To be clear, the file handling provided by C isn't part of the language. It is part of the C standard library of functions and this is mapped onto the native file handing of whatever operating system the program is being run under.

Basic Files

A file is a stream of bytes, but you can regard these bytes as character codes and hence treat the file as text, or you can regard them as raw bytes and treat the file as binary. If you have been following the "everything is a bit pattern" argument, you can see that there isn't a lot of difference between text and binary files.

Before you can work with a file you have to open it. A file may exist somewhere before you open it or it may be created by opening it. Once a file is opened it can be worked on in a program and bytes can be read from it or written to it. Once you have finished working with a file you have to close it. If you don't close a file then it might not be saved properly or the device dealing with it may not work correctly. In practice, if your program terminates normally files will be closed for you, but if it crashes you might not be so lucky. It is the general rule that files that you open are files that you should close and as soon as you can.

The function that is used to open a file is:

```
fptr=fopen("filename","mode");
```

where *filename* is the name of the file and *mode* is how you want to do with the file. The fopen function is defined in stdio.h.

Mode is any of:

r   open for read – returns NULL if file doesn't exist

w   open for write – if the file exists it is overwritten

a   open for append – open file and add data to the end

r+   open for reading and writing – returns NULL if file doesn't exist

w+   open for reading and writing – if the file exists it is overwritten

a+   open for reading and appending – if the file doesn't exist it is created

All of these open the file in text mode if you add a b after the first letter then the file is open for binary processing. For example rb+ opens the file for reading and writing as a binary file.

In most cases there is no real difference between opening for binary or text mode. It is just a matter of what functions you use to read or write the file. However some implementations do make a distinction so if you want to write portable code open a file using the appropriate mode.

When you open a file you are returned a file pointer of type FILE *. If something went wrong then the file pointer is NULL. You use the file pointer to refer to the file in other operations.

For example to close the file you use

```
fclose(fptr);
```

were `fptr` is the file pointer to the file you want to close.

The system defined three standard streams: `stdin` typically the keyboard, `stdout` typically the screen and `stderr` where error messages etc are sent.

Text Mode

If you open a file in text mode then it is very like using `printf` and `scanf` to send characters to the screen and read characters from the keyboard. In fact the equivalent file functions are `fprintf` and `fscanf`.

For example, to write the string "Hello File World" to a file you would use:

```
FILE *f=fopen("myFile.txt","w");
fprintf(f,"Hello File World");
fclose(f);
```

You don't have to use any particular form of filename, but the extension .txt is suggestive that this is indeed a text file.

Of course, you can reopen the file and read the data back:

```
f=fopen("myFile.txt","r");
char text[100];
fscanf(f,"%s",text);
fclose(f);
printf("%s",text);
```

Notice that you can reuse the variable that stores the file pointer. If you try the program you will find that it only prints `Hello` the reason is that `fscanf`, like `scanf`, only reads the input characters until it reaches the first space. |

We have all of the problems we encountered earlier reading data from the keyboard. Of course we do, the keyboard is just another stream of data and the functions that work with it are more or less the same.

You have to be careful not to read too much data and overrun the buffer in exactly the same way. In the case of files on disk or other storage this is usually easier in principle because they are generally written by programs and hence have a fixed format. Even so you have to protect your program from buffer overrun – i.e. you cannot depend on a file format to avoid buffer overrun.

In an earlier chapter we also encountered `fputs` and `fgets` as ways of safely reading and writing strings to a file and these are the best functions to use in most cases. The:

```
fputs(string,fptr);
```

function will write the characters in a string to the file, but it does not write the final `NULL`. It returns `EOF` if there is a problem and a non-negative value otherwise

The function:

```
fgets(string,length,fptr);
```

reads characters from the file until it reaches `length-1` characters or a newline character. The string returned is always null-terminated.

You can see that using `fgets` means that you shouldn't ever overrun a buffer, but to make things work properly you have to arrange to write a newline character to mark the end of the string written to the file.

For example, to write the Hello File World string you would use

```
FILE *f=fopen("myFile.txt","w");
fprintf(f,"Hello File World\n");
fclose(f);
```

which explicitly includes a newline character to mark the end of the string.

You could also use:

```
FILE *f=fopen("myFile.txt","w");
fputs("Hello File World\n",f);
fclose(f);
```

To read this back you could use:

```
f=fopen("myFile.txt","r");
char text[100];
fgets(text,100,f);
fclose(f);
printf("%s",text);
```

Now when you run the program you will see the entire line "Hello File World" as the `fgets` reads to the newline character. Notice that the newline character is not included in the returned string which is null-terminated. Using this approach you cannot overrun the buffer by not finding a newline character.

Text formatted file handling is always a matter of making sure that you write something out using separator and end-of-record markers to allow you to read the data back in and parse it to separate the data. There is an argument that working with text files is difficult and best avoided. However, if the data isn't being generated by you then you might not be able to. The one big advantage of a text file is that it can be read by simple applications such as editors. Binary mode files are quite different and the way that they work is compared to text mode in the next section.

Binary Files

In many ways binary files are easier to understand and work with. A binary file reads and writes bytes that correspond to the bit patterns stored in C variables. There is no conversion of any sort applied. If you write a 4-byte int out to a binary file then the four bytes are written out exactly as they are stored in memory. The same is true when you read the bytes back in.

If you open a file in binary mode then the only two functions you need to know about are:

```
fread(ptrToBuffer, size, number, fptr);
```

and

```
fwrite(ptrToBuffer,size,number,fptr);
```

They work in the same sort of way, but one reads and one writes bytes to the binary file. The number parameter gives the number of "variables" each of size bytes that will be transferred to or from the buffer referenced by ptrToBuffer. The buffer can be an array of the appropriate type. Each function returns the number of "variables" written or read which could be smaller than the number specified.

For example, to write three ints out to a file you would use:

```
int data[3] = {1, 2, 3};
FILE *f = fopen("myFile.bin", "wb");
fwrite(data, 4, 3, f);
fclose(f);
```

Notice that in this case we can simply pass the array name as it decays to a pointer to the array in this situation. You don't have to use any particular extension for the filename but .bin is common. Notice that this only works if int really is four bytes in length.

A more portable way to write this is:

```
fwrite(data, sizeof(int), 3, f);
```

To read the data back in you would use something like:

```
f = fopen("myFile.bin", "rb");
int data2[3];
fread(data2, 4, 3, f);
fclose(f);
printf("%d", data2[0]);
```

Once you get the idea that all that is happening is that the bytes in memory are being written out to disk and then read back in without modification, you should be able to work out the different ways of using this idea.

For example, to write out a single variable you can use:

```
int myData=42;
FILE *f = fopen("myFile.bin", "wb");
fwrite(&myData, sizeof(int), 1, f);
fclose(f);
```

and to read it back in:

```
f = fopen("myFile.bin", "rb");
fread(&myData, sizeof(int), 1, f);
fclose(f);
printf("%d", myData);
```

Notice that when you write out a value using binary mode you get exactly the same value when you read it back in. This isn't necessarily the case if you use text mode, when the value might be converted to a decimal representation before being converted back to binary when read in. Also notice that text mode can use many more bytes to represent the value.

Structs as Records

When you are working with binary files you have to establish and stick to a very regular format. Usually the simplest way to do this is to create a struct that has the data you want to save and load and make use of this to structure your file.

For example, a record might consist of a name and age. A suitable struct would be:

```
struct person {
    char name[25];
    int age;
};
```

To write a single record out to file:

```
struct person me;
strcpy(me.name,"Harry");
me.age = 18;
FILE *f = fopen("myFile.bin", "wb");
fwrite(&me, sizeof (struct person), 1, f);
fclose(f);
```

To read the data back:

```
struct person me2;
f = fopen("myFile.bin", "rb");
fread(&me2, sizeof (struct person), 1, f);
fclose(f);
printf("%s  %d", me2.name, me2.age);
```

Notice that the struct is treated as a single entity and all of the bytes it uses are written to the file and then read back in.

You can, of course, write multiple records and read multiple records back in one at a time if you want. The key idea is that rather than trying to structure the file by writing variables of different types it is much easier to create a suitable struct and read and write it as a single unit.

Buffering

I/O to `stdout` and `stdin` file streams is generally buffered. If you don't know this you can be surprised by what happens. Buffering isn't as much of a problem with files because you generally don't implement an interaction between reading and writing as you do with a keyboard and screen.

You can force a file to write the data that it has in the buffer using:

```
fflush(fptr);
```

Usually this isn't a good idea unless you are finished with the file and want to make sure it is up-to-date before closing it at a later time. Of course closing the file automatically flushes the buffers.

When a file corresponds to an external device, a sensor say, then in most cases the system will notice and avoid using a buffer but this isn't always the case and you might need to flush the buffer frequently.

There are functions that you can use to control buffering but often these are ignored by particular drivers.

Character I/O

Occasionally you need to treat the stream of bytes from a file as if it was a sequence of characters. In this case the data is generally fairly unstructured and you are typically looking for particular substrings or you are generating free form text such as HTML.

The character handling functions are fairly simple:

```
fputc(charAsint,fptr);
putc(charAsint, fptr);
```

write a single character specified as an `int` to the file. Both functions do the same job but `putc` is generally faster.

Similarly

```
fgetc(fptr);
getc(fptr);
```

retrieve a single character but as an int.

Why as an `int` and not a `char`?

The answer is that the functions return an EOF value if the end of the file has been reached or if there has been an error and this is outside of the range of char. What this means is that you have to test for EOF before you cast to char.

That is:

```
int temp;
char c;
temp=getc(fprt);
if (temp!=EOF) c=(char)temp;
```

Another common situation is the need to read a character to determine what to do next but re-read the character as part of the input to be processed.

For example, suppose you want to discard space characters. The simplest algorithm is to read until you get a non-space character but that non-space character is part of the next word. To make this really simple you can use:

```
ungetc(charAsint,fptr);
```

which will put the character specified back into the buffer as if it had not been read.

For example, to read to the first non-space character:

```
f = fopen("myFile.txt", "r");
int c;
do
     c = getc(f);
while (c == " ");
ungetc(c, f);
```

Now when you read from the file the first character retrieved is the one that was pushed back into the buffer. Notice that this does not alter the file, it only affects the buffer. Different implementations allow different numbers of ungetc commands to work. GNU for example only allows one ungetc. Also any other commands that change the current position in the buffer will cause the character to be lost.

Positioning Functions

When you open a file the reading or writing position is at the start of the file. As you read or write, the file pointer to the current position in the file moves to the next byte to be read or written. This is what a sequential file is all about – reading and writing one byte after another. Originally files were stored on magnetic tape and you worked from the start to the end of the tape. If you wanted to reread the tape or to read what you had just written then you had the tape rewound. You can also rewind a general C file using the function:

```
rewind(fptr);
```

this moves the file position pointer to the start of the file.

Not all streams can be rewound or positioned. Usually files that are stored on disk or similar allow positioning and these are generally referred to as random access files.

More generally you can move to any position in the file using:

```
fseek(fptr,offset,whence);
```

where `offset` is the number of bytes you want to move the pointer by and `whence` is the location that the offset is measured from. If `whence` is `SEEK_SET` then `offset` is from the start of the file, if it is `SEEK_CUR` it is from the current location and if it is `SEEK_END` it is from the end of the file. The function returns `0` if the seek worked.

You can find out where the position pointer is using:

```
ftell(fptr);
```

which returns the position or `-1` if the stream doesn't have a position.

For POSIX systems `ftell` and `fseek` work for both binary and text files. In non-compatible systems they may only be trustworthy for binary files. For text files the best that you can do is to use `ftell` to retrieve a position and then use that value in `fseek` to move back to that position.

End Of File Errors

If you try to read beyond the current end of a file then the file functions return an `EOF` value, which is usually `-1`. The problem is that they also return `EOF` for file errors. To test for a true EOF you need to use:

```
feof(fptr);
```

which returns a non-zero value if the file is positioned at the end of file.

You can also use:

```
ferror(fptr);
```

which returns a non-zero value for a general file error.

Note that fseeking beyond the end of the file does not trigger an `EOF`. In fact a seek clears any `EOF` flags that have been set.

Random Access

What you can do with a file when you are using `fseek` depends on how the file was opened.

If the file was opened exclusively for reading then you can move around the file, successfully reading whatever bytes you care to and interpreting them in whatever way you want to. You can also re-read any part of the file as often as you need to. It is also obvious that the set position has to be between the start and the end of the file.

If the file was opened exclusively for writing then you can move to a position that has already been written or to the end of the file where new data can be added to extend the file. On POSIX-compliant systems you can also move beyond the `EOF` and write data there. The data between the end of file and the newly written data will be read as zeros. This is not part of any C standard which instead specifies that you can rewrite data as many times as you like, but that you can only add new data to the end of the file.

Things get a tiny bit more complicated if the file is open for both reading and writing. In this case you can still rewrite existing data and add new data to the end of the file. If it is POSIX-compliant then you can also `fseek` beyond the end of the file. However if you switch between reading and writing you have to take account of the effects of buffering. Essentially if you move from writing to reading you have to make sure that the buffer is flushed. The C99 standard says that if you follow a write by a read then there has to be an intervening call to `fflush`, `fseek`, `fsetpos` or `rewind`. Switching from reading to writing is easier but you still need a call to `fseek`, `fsetpos` or `rewind` first unless you are already at the end-of-file. If you do immediately follow a write by a read or a read by a write then you trigger undefined behavior.

Opening a file for read and write and using positioning functions makes it easy to create a record oriented random access file – a simple database.

The idea is that you write a file of records based on a `struct`. For example, to write out ten name and age records you might use:

```
struct person me;
strcpy(me.name, "Harry");
me.age = 18;

FILE *f = fopen("myFile.bin", "wb+");

for (int i = 0; i < 10; i++) {
    fwrite(&me, sizeof (struct person), 1, f);
    me.age++;
};
fflush(f);
```

As we are writing consecutive records, no file positioning is needed and notice that each record is a year older so that you can check which record is read.

Now suppose you want to read the fifth record. This is obviously stored at an offset from the start of the file of 5*sizeof(struct person) and this is how you can move the file position to the correct location before reading the struct:

```
int record = 5;
fseek(f, record * sizeof (struct person), SEEK_SET);
struct person me2;
fread(&me2, sizeof (struct person), 1, f);
printf("%s  %d", me2.name, me2.age);
```

You can use the same technique to position the file for a write to update a record. A modify is implemented by reading the record changing the value and then writing it again but notice that you need to position the file again to avoid undefined behavior:

```
fseek(f, record * sizeof (struct person), SEEK_SET);
read(&me2, sizeof (struct person), 1, f);
me2.age++;
fseek(f, record * sizeof (struct person), SEEK_SET);
fwrite(&me2, sizeof (struct person), 1, f);
```

Notice that the fseek before the fwrite is logically needed to position the file back to the start of the record after reading it. File reading and writing is always sequential after a positioning.

New records are added by simply moving the end of the file and writing. On a POSIX system you can also add a record beyond the end of the file and the missing records will be read as zeros until real data is written. For example:

```
fseek(f, 25 * sizeof (struct person), SEEK_SET);
fwrite(&me, sizeof (struct person), 1, f);
```

writes a record at the 25th position, filling in the gap with zeros. That is, if you read record 24 the string will be a null string and the age will be zero.

This is all fine if you only want to find a record by a sequential record number, but what if you want to find a record by the value in a field? To implement this you need a lookup table that stores the field value and the record number that gives its location in the file. This lookup table is often created as another file which is read into memory for efficiency and is generally called an index. You can continue this line of thought until you have implemented a database, but it is usually a lot less work to make use of, or even modify, an existing database program.

The important point is that you can see how easy it is to use a random access file to store, retrieve and update data.

File Operations

Reading and writing files are fairly standard operations, but operating systems provide many other ways to manipulate files including permissions, passwords and so on. These are not so easy to standardize. C includes a small number of additional functions that manipulate files, including:

```
remove(filename);
```

which makes the file inaccessible. In most cases this means it deletes the file but exactly what happens isn't defined.

```
rename(oldfilename,newfilename);
```

which renames the file. What happens if *newfilename* already exists or if *oldfilename* doesn't exist depends on the implementation.

The function:

```
tmpfile();
```

returns a file pointer to a temporary file that is created without you having to worry about its name or potential name clashes. The file is opened in wb+ mode and is automatically removed when you close it.

The function:

```
tmpnam(string);
```

returns a file name that is guaranteed not to clash with an existing name. The generated file name is stored in the string argument which must have TEMP_MAX characters.

If you are working with a Unix like POSIX based operating system you will find that there are many more file handling functions defined in unistd.h. This is where you will discover how to set working directories, symbolic links, and file attributes and more. If you know the Linux file handling command you are need to use then there will be a function of the same or similar name and usage.

Sharing Files – Locking

Files, or more generally streams, are sometimes used as a communication channel between different processes, different programs and even different machines. The idea is that a file can be read and written by more than one agent. If files are shared then there is the problem of simultaneous update. The solution is to use a lock to restrict who can access it. There are locking functions provided by POSIX but they aren't reliable and a much better solution is to use general resource locking mechanisms. You will also encounter the idea of a lock file. This is just a dummy file that is tested for to determine if another process has the file open already. These topics are covered in *Applying C For The IoT With Linux* ISBN: 978-1871962611.

232

Summary

- If you think of a file as just a sequence or stream of bytes that can be read or written then you have an idea that fits a great many sources and sinks of data.

- This idea is so powerful that under Linux/Unix you can view almost all data as an example of a file.

- C has a standard way of working with files – streams – and it provides a range of functions for working with file pointers such as fopen and fclose.

- In text mode a C file can be accessed using fprintf and fscanf which are file versions of printf and scanf.

- In binary mode you can use fread and fwrite to work with binary data as sets of bytes.

- The natural way to organize binary files is to use structs as if they were records.

- C files are buffered and this can cause unexpected behavior. Use fflush to make sure that buffers are written out.

- You can also use lower level character functions fgetc and fputc.

- Files are read from the current position which can be changed using rewind or fseek. You can find the current position using ftell.

- Detecting the end of a file is sometimes difficult as EOF is returned if there is an error as well as when the end of file has been reached.#

- Using file positioning and structs it is very easy to implement a simple database.

- There are a range of file manipulation commands that allow you to do things like rename files.

- Linux/Unix file locking is troublesome and it is better to implement your own locking from first principles.

Chapter 14

Compiling C - Preprocessor, Compiler, Linker

So far we have mostly ignored the process of turning a C program into an executable. In the case of many languages this is a trivial process – the system runs the program. In the case of C things are more complicated for a variety of reasons. The main difference is that C has a preprocessor which is generally thought of as some sort of text processing engine that can transform your source code before it is presented to the compiler. The preprocessor should not be underestimated as in the early days it was the tool that converted C++ into C, so avoiding the need for a C++ compiler. At the very least you need to understand it and the way header files are combined with code files to create the document that is submitted to the compiler.

We also need to look at the process of converting source code into an executable. This is a more involved process than you might think and to fully master the C environment you need to understand it.

Up to this point we have avoided having to consider how everything works because we have relied on NetBeans to get the job done. NetBeans hides much of the complexity from the beginner, but sooner or later you have to find out where your files are and how it all works. This doesn't mean you have to give up using an IDE like NetBeans, but you will understand what it is doing much better.

Four Stages of Compilation

When you compile a C program there are four distinct stages:

- ◆ Preprocessing
- ◆ Compilation
- ◆ Assembly
- ◆ Linking

These stages all happen when the GCC compiler is invoked – so it isn't really just the compiler you are using. Other compilers do the job in similar ways, but for the sake of concrete examples let's focus on GCC.

Your C program takes the form of a text file, usually with a name like `myprogram.c`, where you write not just the C language but instructions to the preprocessor about how to modify the file. In particular the `#include` statements that you have been using are instructions to the preprocessor to merge additional files together with yours to produce the final text file that will be submitted to the compiler. This merged file is usually called a unit of compilation and it has the same name as your source file but with a different extension, e.g. `myprogram.i`.

The compiler takes the unit of compilation and produces an intermediate file with the same name as your source code and another extension, e.g. `myprogram.s`. This contains assembly code. That is, the compiler doesn't compile to machine code, but to assembler. You can view and edit the assembly language that the compiler produces.

The intermediate file is processed by an assembler to produce machine code in a file with the same name as your source code with yet another extension, e.g. `myprogram.o`.

You might think that this is the end of the story and now you can run the machine code as an executable program, but this is usually not the case. The program generally is missing code that performs initialization and it may well refer to functions that are not defined in the compilation unit. Your code can refer to functions such as `printf`, which aren't part of your program but are defined in libraries. The libraries are precompiled and are available as files ending in `.o`. The linker takes your `.o` file and either adds the code of the library function to it, static linking, or creates a reference to the external code, dynamic linking.

Static linking is simple, but the code is included in your executable program and having `printf` included in every executable in a system would make the code much bigger. Dynamic linking allows programs to share the library definition and hence save space, but if the library is missing your program will not run. Your program has a dependency on the library.

At last you have an executable that can be run. The linker outputs the final machine code file that is your executable and it uses a name with yet another extension. In the case of GCC this is usually a null extension, so your executable in this example is `myprogram`.

Thus the sequence is:

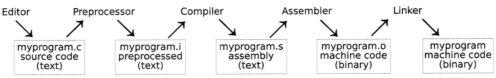

We now need to look at the details of some of these steps.

The Preprocessor - Include

The preprocessor is a powerful tool but it is also a dangerous one unless you fully realize that it is just a text processor.

The simplest thing that the preprocessor does for you is read in and merge include files.

When the preprocessor encounters:

```
#include "myfile"
```

it finds myfile and replaces the line with the contents of the file.

All preprocessor instructions start with a hash symbol and don't end with a semicolon.

By convention files that are intended to be included have the extension .h and files that are not intended to be included have the extension .c but they are all C source files. You can include files with other extensions. There is more to say about header files and how they are used after we have looked at the linker.

The GCC compiler automatically searches for header files in the same directory as the source file and then in standard system directories, usually:

```
/usr/local/include/
/usr/include/
```

but this isn't fixed. You can also include a relative path for the include file.

For example:

```
#include "mysub/myfile.h"
```

will first look in the folder mysub in the current directory.

If you use the angle bracket form:

```
#include <myfile>
```

then only the system folders are searched.

You can add directories to the search path using the -I command line option. If you are using NetBeans then you can set additional include directories using the project properties.

Going beyond #include the key idea is that of a macro, indeed the preprocessor is best defined as a macro processor.

Macros

You define a macro using:

```
#define macroname string
```

Anywhere the preprocessor finds *macroname* it replaces it by the string. It is convention to use all caps for the name of the macro to make its status clear. You can write the macro on multiple lines using the \ line break but the it is treated as if it was defined on a single line.

For example:

```
#define ONEHUNDRED 100
int x=ONEHUNDRED;
```

is expanded to:

```
int x=100;
```

You can see the expanded macro by running the preprocessor from the command line:

```
cpp myprogram.c
```

the result is an `.i` file that you can inspect.

If you are using NetBeans then a simpler option is to right-click on a macro and select `Navigate,View Macro Expansion`. This opens the Macro Expansion window where you can view the result of the expansion of all of the macros in a program.

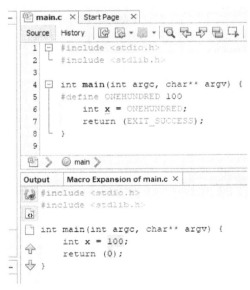

238

The simplest use of a macro is to define constants such as:

```
#define PI 3.14159
```

Macros take effect after they have been defined – the preprocessor reads the file from top to bottom, expanding macros as it goes.

There is also the instruction:

```
#undefine
```

which undefines a macro. This can be useful if you want the definition of a macro to apply only to part of the program or if you need different definitions in different parts of the program.

Notice that this macro replaces any use of PI by the number 3.14159 as if you had typed it into the text file. Compare this to the use of a const variable.

You can use parameters within macros to create a function macro. The parameters are a comma-separated list within parentheses. You have to write the parentheses hard against the macro's name otherwise the parameters are taken to be part of the string that defines the macro body.

For example:

```
#define PI(n) 3.14159*n
```

If you use this in an expression it is as if you had written out the equivalent text. That is:

```
int x=PI(2);
```

is exactly equivalent to:

```
int x=3.14159*2;
```

Notice that macros don't have any idea of data type. You can just as well write:

```
int x=PI(rotation);
```

and this would be exactly equivalent to:

```
int x=3.14159*rotation;
```

Notice that the macro is expanded as a string which is inserted into your program as if you had typed it. In this case the instruction that results is legal as long as rotation has been declared as a suitable variable earlier in the program.

You can have multiple parameters and you have to specify them all as a comma-separated list when you use the macro. Any parameters that you don't specify are treated as blank. Any parameters that you include in quotes are not treated as parameters.

For example:

```
#define PI(n) "n times Pi"
```

expands to "n times Pi", including the quotes, no matter what n is.

As long as you always think about macros as simple text substitution and nothing more you will likely not make mistakes – or rather you will understand why you make mistakes.

For example:

```
#define MUL(A,B) A*B
```

works fine in simple cases:

```
int x=MUL(2,3);
```

and expands to:

```
int x= 2*3;
```

Consider, however, what happens if you are more adventurous:

```
int x=MUL(a+2,b+3);
```

Due to operator precedence, this expands to:

```
int x=a+2*b+3;
```

which is presumably not what was intended.

This problem of operator precedence is the reason why macros often seem to have lots of extra parentheses. For example the MUL macro is better defined as:

```
#define MUL(A,B) (A)*(B)
```

The parentheses look redundant, but they make sure that whatever A is and whatever B is they are evaluated before the multiplication.

In general, many problems with macros occur because other programmers use arguments you never intended your macro to be used with.

Now we come to a feature of macros that can cause even more problems. When a macro is expanded the result is inserted into the file in place of macroname. The preprocessor then re-scans that portion of text and expands any macros it finds. The same is true if an argument contains a macro, when the macro is expanded and placed within the argument.

For example:

```
#define SUM(A,B) (A)+(B)
```

now we can write:

```
int x=SUM(MUL(x,y),z);
```

and this expands first to:

```
int x=SUM((x)*(y),z);
```

and then to:

```
int x=((x)*(y))+(z);
```

which, despite having too many parentheses, is perfectly correct.

At this point you might be thinking that macros can be recursive and hence the preprocessor has the power of a full language. This is not the case. Any self reference within a macro is ignored, i.e. it is treated as text and not expanded. This also applies if the self reference is via another macro.

So if you define:

```
#define ADDONE ADDONE+1
```

the statement:

```
int x=ADDONE;
```

expands to

```
int x=ADDONE+1;
```

and not to an infinite recursion.

Finally the #, or stringizing operator, converts a parameter into a string constant, i.e. a quoted string, without expanding it. For example:

```
#define MKSTRING(s) #s
printf(MKSTRING(Hello World));
```

expands to

```
printf("Hello World");
```

The ## token-pasting operator allows concatenation of parameters. In this case the arguments are expanded before being concatenated. For example:

```
#define CREATSTRUCT(type,name) type name; type##* name##p
CREATSTRUCT(struct mystruct,myvar);
```

expands to:

```
struct mystruct myvar;
struct mystruct* myvarp;
```

Notice that we use ## to add the p to the end of the variable name to create a pointer.

There are also predefined macros that implement things that would be difficult without them. For example __FILE__, __LINE__ and __DATE__ expand to the current file name, line number and date respectively. The only way to find out what your system supports is to consult the manual.

Macros are useful, but they are not as powerful as you might imagine and they quickly become dangerous.

There are extensions to the basic macro syntax that are only supported by particular C standards. For example, C99 supports a variable number of parameters.

The C preprocessor's syntax doesn't seem to have much to do with C so it is easy to forget that it is actually defined by the C standards. The problem is that it isn't particularly well defined by them and hence there are variations in how things work. The best advice is to keep macros simple and only to use the most common idioms.

You also will encounter unexpected problems even with simple macros – usually because of the way spaces are either inserted or not inserted, the way punctuation modifies meaning, and the range of things that can be passed as arguments.

It is worth saying that you will encounter macros in code that leave you wondering what they do and how they work. Such macros are best avoided and are not to be admired or emulated.

Conditional Compilation

The preprocessor has another major use in addition to includes and macros – conditional compilation, which enables a number of conditional directives to be evaluated at compile time.

The most basic of these are:

```
#ifdef MACRO
text
#endif
```

If the macro is defined then all of the *text* between the `ifdef` and `endif` is included in the output file. If the macro isn't defined than the *text* is skipped. The *text* can even contain macros and these will be expanded if *text* is included. Also notice that *text* has to expand to valid C.

There is also:

```
#ifndef MACRO
```

which works in the same way but *text* is included if the macro isn't defined.

You can also use:

```
#else
```

and

```
#elif
```

to create the familiar conditional structures.

For example:

```
#if ARM
int processor=1;
#else
int processor=2;
#endif
```

If you have defined the macro `ARM` then the source file contains the line:

```
int processor=1;
```

if the macro isn't defined then the source file contains the line:

```
int processor=2;
```

The only difficulty is in keeping in mind that all of these conditionals are evaluated when the preprocessor runs, i.e. before the compiler, and that they are all text modifications.

A very common use of conditional compilation is to make sure that a header file is only actually included once, no matter how many times the programmer includes it:

```
#ifndef MYHEADER
#define MYHEADER
text of header file
#endif
```

The first time the header file is included, `MYHEADER` is not defined so the whole text of the header file is added to the source code. The second and subsequent times the header is included, `MYHEADER` is defined and so its text is not added to the source code.

Most of the time you can rely on just using `#ifdef` but there is a more sophisticated conditional:

```
#if expression
```

where *expression* is an integer C expression with some restrictions. You can use addition, subtraction, multiplication, division, bitwise operations, shifts, comparisons, and logical operations, but only with integer and character constants – the value of any variable that you use obviously cannot be known until runtime. If you do use an identifier that isn't a macro then it is treated as zero. You can also use macros within the expression and these will be expanded before the expression is evaluated.

The operator:

```
defined(MACRO)
```

is useful in that it is true, i.e. 1, if `MACRO` is defined.

One of the main uses of #if is to test for combinations of macros to be defined.

For example:

```
#if defined(ARM) && defined(BIGRAM)
```

will only include its text if both ARM and BIGRAM are defined.

You can see that conditional compilation is useful when you need to tailor your code to different systems, but it can also be useful if you want to include optional features, e.g. debugging code.

Another common use of conditional compilation is to comment out a block of code. You might think that surrounding the code by /* */ would do the job, but any block comments within the code being commented out would cancel the outer comment as comments don't nest. A simple solution is to surround the block with:

```
#if 0
text to be removed
#endif
```

This is safer than using ifdef as the macro might be undefined by another part of the program. Notice that this also works if the text contains conditionals as it isn't included and hence never expanded or processed.

Linking

After the preprocessor has finished, the compiler transforms the expanded C code into the assembler of the target machine. The machine-specific assembler then translates this to machine code. These two steps are major undertakings, but from the programmer's point of view mostly invisible. It is sometimes interesting to look at the assembly language output of the compiler to see how the C code is being interpreted, but it is rare that you need to get involved in either step other than setting optimization levels for the compiler as command line options.

The machine code that the assembler outputs usually isn't complete and runable. It lacks the boilerplate startup code and it lacks any code that that has been referenced in a library. The linker's job is to add the missing code to the output of the assembler to create a final executable file.

From the programmer's point of view the most important aspect of the Linker is the way it takes code from the libraries that you have specified and "links" it together to form the final executable. Clearly if the linker cannot find the library file then the compile fails.

Library files come in two types, archive files ending `.a` or shared object files ending `.so`. Archive files are statically linked into your program i.e. their code is read into the final executable. Shared object files are dynamically linked and their code is stored in the library file which is accessed by your executable when it is run.

One of the biggest problems is specifying where library files are. GCC will invoke the linker as a final step and this will search for libraries in several standard directories, usually:

```
/usr/local/lib/
/usr/lib/
```

You can specify additional library directories using the `-L` compiler option or you can specify them using the project properties in NetBeans. This is very similar to the way that you can specify search paths for include files, however, in the case of link libraries you also have to specify the names of the library files using the `-l` (lower case) option or by using Project Properties in NetBeans. The `-l` option assumes that the name of the library starts with `LIB` and has a `.a` extension. So `-lmylib` looks for a library file called `LIBmylib.a` in the library directories including any you have added using `-L`. If you want to specify a non-standard name use a leading colon e.g. `-l:mylib.o` looks for the file `mylib.o` in the library directories.

There is often some confusion about the relationship between header files and library files. If you want to use a library then usually you have to include its header file. Surely this is enough to tell the compiler what you want it to do? Unfortunately not. The header file simply tells the compiler what functions etc the library contains so that you can use them without the compiler complaining that you have used things you haven't declared. However, the compiler doesn't generate the code for the library functions and it doesn't even fill in the details of how the functions are called. It simply leaves a stub function call which the linker has to fill in when it locates the function in the library you specify.

What this means is that if you leave out the include file the compiler will complain when you use library functions. If you have an include file the compiler will be happy, but if the linker cannot find the library file to complete the function calls then your final executable will not be complete and will not work.

The best way to make sure you understand all of this is to create your own libraries and make use of them.

A Static Library

Creating libraries for your own use is surprisingly easy and it is a good way to make your code reusable and particularly reusable by others.

The basic steps to create a library are:

1. Create the C code for your library file.
2. Create a header file that defines the functions and resources in your library.
3. Compile the C code to create a .o file
4. Make the .o file and the .h file available for use.

The basic steps in using a library you already know, but for completeness:

1. Include the .h file
2. Add the .o library file to the linker
3. Use the functions in the library as if they were part of your program.

One small complication is that, as well as .o object files that can be used as libraries, there are also .a or archive files which are more commonly used. An archive file can store multiple object files in a compressed format. This has the advantage that you can build a large library from multiple object files each developed separately in its own .c file. What this means is that in practice step 3 usually involves creating an archive file from the object file.

First we need a C implementation of some functions. The simplest example is to provide some mathematical functions. Start a new C project and add a second C file to it called MySumLib and enter the following lines:

```c
float Pi=3.14159;
int add(int a,int b){
    return a+b;
}
int mul(int a,int b){
    return a*b;
}
```

There are a number of different ways of creating a library file using NetBeans including a special project type, but using a standard project means you get a main function which you can use to test your library.

If you build this project you will discover that there is a MySumLib.o file in the build/debug directory. The exact name of this directory changes according to the build server you are using but it is easy enough to find. You can use this object file as your library file.

Next we have to create a suitable header file. Add a header file to the project called `MySumLIB.h` and enter the following lines:

```
#ifndef MYSUMLIB_H
#define MYSUMLIB_H
extern float Pi;
extern int add(int,int);
extern int mul(int,int);
#endif /* MYSUMLIB_H */
```

The lines involving `MYSUMLIB_H` are generated by NetBeans and they are the standard way of avoiding including the same header file more than once. The three lines that we have entered define the variable Pi and the two functions `add` and `mul`. The keyword `extern` tells the compiler that these declarations are actually defined in some other file i.e. they are external to the current file. The memory that the variables and the functions use is allocated by the code in the library file not the main program using them. However, the main program needs to know what the externs "look like" i.e. what type `Pi` is.

Remember the header file is going to be used in a program that is using the library and it tells the compiler that `Pi`, `add` and `mul` are defined elsewhere and will be resolved by the linker.

Now we need a program to use the library. Start a new project and enter:

```
#include <stdio.h>
#include <stdlib.h>

#include "../MyMathLib/MySumLIB.h"

int main(int argc, char** argv) {
    printf("%f\n",Pi);
    printf("%d\n", add(2, 3));
    printf("%d\n",mul(2,3));

    return (EXIT_SUCCESS);
}
```

If you enter the program without the `MySumLib.h` file then the compiler will complain that it doesn't know about `Pi`, `sum` or `mul`. If you include it then the compiler is happy but the linker will complain later that it cannot find them. The solution is to tell the linker where the missing library is, and this is often the most difficult part. You could copy the library file to one of the standard library directories but while you are testing and developing it makes sense to leave it where it has been created.

Use the program properties and the linker section to set a new library directory i.e. the -L option:

```
../mylibtest/build/Debug/GNU-Linux
```

and the library file name:

```
:MySumLib.o
```

The colon is needed because this is not a library with a standard name such as `libname.a`.

The command line is now:

```
gcc  -o dist/Debug/GNU-Linux/uselib build/Debug/GNU-Linux/main.o
 -L../mylibtest/build/Debug/GNU-Linux -l:MySumLib.o
```

Now if you run the program you should see everything work.

This is a simple example and it works, but it isn't the way things are usually done. The first change is that a static library like the one we have just created is usually packaged as an archive file. This is a matter of using the archiver `ar`. As the directory path to the object files created by NetBeans tends to be deep, the simplest thing to do is to use a GUI file manager to drag-and-drop MySumLib.o to your home directory and then use the command, you can use the NetBeans remote terminal:

```
ar rcs libsum.a MySumLib.o
```

This packs `MySumLib.o` into the archive file `libsum.a`. You can pack multiple object files into the same library file by continuing the command with their filenames separated by spaces.

Finally if you copy `libsub.a` back to the original directory you can use the add library file to the linker but as it is now in standard format you can specify its name as `sum`. The command line is:

```
gcc -o dist/Debug/GNU-Linux/uselib build/Debug/GNU-Linux/main.o
 -L../mylibtest/build/Debug/GNU-Linux -lsum
```

If you are using NetBeans then there is a quicker way to generate an archive file. Instead of creating a new C Application create a Static Library project. This lacks a main function and you have to add your own C files and header files to create the library. When you build the project, you can't run it as there is no `main` function, the compiler creates an archive file for you in the directory:

```
dist/Debug/GNU-Linux
```

or similar. This means you can use the archive file after the build without any additional steps.

You can also convert the existing project into a static library project using Properties, Build, Configuration Type and setting it to Static Library.

Notice that you have created a static library and this means that the code in the library will be included in your executable. There is no need to distribute the library to end users – it is in your executable. However, sometimes is is a good idea to create a shared library to avoid the overhead in packaging the static library into every executable.

248

Creating a Dynamic Library

A shared file has the extension `.so` and it is created in much the same way. From the command line you simply add `-shared` and make sure that the name of the output file ends in `.so`.

For example:

```
gcc -shared -o libsum.so mylib.c
```

If you are using NetBeans then a simpler option is to create a Dynamic Library project. You can also use the properties Build Configuration and select Dynamic Library. When you build the project a `.so` file is created in:

```
dist/Debug/GNU-Linux
```

Using the shared library is just as easy as using a static library. Specify the path and the library file using the `-L` and `-l` command line options or the Properties, Build, Linker dialog. Everything works in the same way as for a static file only now you will find that the program compiles, but when you try to run it you will get a runtime error informing you that the library cannot be found. Shared libraries not only need to be findable during the linking phase, but at runtime the dynamic linker has to be able to find them as well and this is something of a problem.

The simplest solution, and the preferred one, is to copy the shared library into either `/usr/lib` or `/usr/local/lib` and then use the `ldconfig` command to set up the dynamic linker. A less foolproof method is to set an environment variable that the dynamic linker uses to find the library. To do this in NetBeans select the project properties and in `Run, Environment` add `Name LD_LIBRARY_PATH` and value *path to library*. Again, as NetBeans uses a long and complex path to the `dist` directory, it is easier to move the `.so` file to an easier directory.

When you first discover shared libraries they seem like a really good idea, but in practice there are lots of problems. Windows programmers often refer to DLL hell for the problems that arise from trying to keep a shared library ecosystem up-to-date. The problem is that the shared library can be updated independently of the programs that make use of it and can even be rendered binary-incompatible with previous versions of the programs. Static libraries produce robust applications that don't depend on the current version of a shared library. In most cases it is worth spending the extra memory on not having to share a library for the simplicity it brings.

Make

When you first start creating programs you can keep everything together in one file and compile it in one operation. As your program gets bigger, the time to compile increases and you are bound to notice that you are performing a huge compile to account for changes in a few lines – perhaps just one.

The solution is to break the program down into small compilation units and arrange to only compile the units that have changed. The final program is then created by linking together the object files, but using existing object files for any that haven't been changed. You could arrange to do this manually, but as a programmer you are probably going to invent a way to automate the process. The good news is you don't have to as it has already been done several times. The best known such system is GNU make and most C programs are actually compiled and linked using a make file. Even if you are using NetBeans, the actual process of building your program is done using a make file that has been automatically constructed for you. As long as you are happy to let NetBeans do this job, you can ignore make files, but sooner or later something will go wrong or you will need something special and a knowledge of how it all works is a good idea.

A make file is a list of rules for making your program. There may be multiple sets of rules for making different versions of the program, but for the moment let's keep things simple and create a single target. A rule is the name of a target, usually the name of a file that is to be generated, a list of prerequisites, files that are needed to make the target, and a list of recipes that generally use the *prerequisites* to create the *Target*.

```
Target : prerequisites
        recipe1
        recipe2
        ...
```

Each line of the recipes has to start with a tab character for historical reasons.

So far this just looks like a program to automate the creation of a program, but there are two extra features that you need to keep in mind if you are going to understand what a particular make file actually does.

- The first is that the *target* is only made using the recipes if at least one of the *prerequisites* is newer than any current *target* file. That is, if the *target* file already exists and its creation date is equal to or newer than all of the *prerequisite* files then nothing happens.

- The second is that a *prerequisite* file can be the *target* in another rule. A make file is organized so that if you just run it then the first rule encountered is acted on, but any rules that have a *prerequisite* as a *target* are evaluated before the first rules recipes are run.

These two features work together to make a make file more sophisticated than you might first think.

For example:

```
myprog: main.o mylib.o
        gcc -o myprog main.o mylib.o
main.o: main.c mylib.h
        gcc -c main.c
mylib.o: mylib.c
        gcc -c mylib.c
```

The first rule is for the myprog target and the prerequisites are the two object files that the recipe uses, main.o and mylib.o. The recipe uses GCC to link the object files together to make the executable. Before it does this, however, it checks to see if any of the prerequisites are the targets of subsequent rules – and you can see that they both are.

The rule for main.o has prerequisites main.c and main.h neither of these are targets of later rules so the creation dates are compared. If main.c and main.h are older or the same age as main.o the recipe is ignored and the current main.o is left untouched. If either are newer then the recipe is used to make a new main.o.

The same thing happens for mylib.o and it is either left alone or remade if mylib.c is newer.

At this point the attention switches back to the first rule and now the creation date of myprog is compared to main.o and mylib.o. If either of them is newer then myprog is remade using the compiler to link the object files together.

You can see from this that a make file isn't just a set of instructions for building the target, it implements an intelligent build that only does work where it is necessary to take account of the files that have changed since the last time the build occurred. Also notice that how intelligent this build is depends on the way you structure the rules.

You might think that the above make file was equivalent to:

```
myprog: main.c mylib.c
        gcc -o myprog main.c mylib.c
```

but this simpler version only checks the creation dates of main.c and mylib.c and performs a complete build if either are newer than myprog, i.e. both object files are recreated if only one has changed.

There are lots of additional features that increase the ease of use of make. For example, you can use variables:

```
objects= main.o mylib.o
```

and to include the value of a variable you can use $(*var*) or ${*var*}. So the start of our example could be written:

```
myprog: $(objects)
        gcc -o myprog $(objects)
```

You can also include one make file within another using the include directive.

It is worth knowing that you can select a target by using it on the command line. For example:

```
make myprog
```

runs the rule with myprog as a target.

You can also create a rule that doesn't have a file as a target by using a phony rule with the rule you want as a prerequisite. The standard example is:

```
clean:
        rm myprog $(objects)
```

which will remove the program and the object files when you use:

```
make clean
```

The problem is, what if there is a file called clean in the directory? Then the recipe will never be used because the file is always up-to-date. To avoid this you use:

```
.PHONY : clean
clean:
        rm myprog $(objects)
```

These are the basic ideas of a make file but things can quickly get complicated – especially so for automatically generated make files. For example, NetBeans uses a make file to build your project and it is tens of lines long. The make file that is included in the important files part of the project has lots of targets that you can use to include custom build steps. The actual make file the builds the program is stored elsewhere and included in the one you get to see. You also need to remember that a recipe can be any valid shell commands including for loops and if statements. Make files can be complicated, but this introduction should allow you to understand generated make files and those hand-crafted by other programmers.

Conclusion

After earlier chapters in which we've looked at the fundamental requirements for writing code in the C language, in this one we've followed how the code becomes an executable program. This brings to a close this preliminary exploration of C and you should now feel able to write C programs and modify existing ones. However, there is still a lot to learn. In particular, if you want to know more about using C on POSIX-compliant and Linux-based systems, for low level, IoT or embedded applications then see this book's companion volume: *Applying C For The IoT With Linux* ISBN: 978-1871962611.

Summary

- When you compile a C program there are four distinct stages: Preprocessing, Compilation, Assembly and Linking.

- The C preprocessor can be used to modify C source code using macros. It is important to keep in mind that everything that the preprocessor does is about text manipulation.

- The include command can be used to read in files into the compilation unit.

- More generally macros can be used to define constants and implement conditional compilation.

- Linking is the process whereby any unresolved function calls are resolved by loading code from libraries.

- Library files come in two forms – static and dynamic.

- A static library contains functions which are added to your code as needed. This means that your code contains a copy of the function and this can make its executable larger than necessary.

- A dynamic library is shared among all the programs that use it. This saves storage, but the executable has to be able to find the library when it runs. There is also the problem of updates to shared library files breaking the programs that make use of them.

- Make is a batch file processor that makes compiling more efficient by only processing those files that have changed since the last time the program was compiled.

Index

259

Other Books by Harry Fairhead

Applying C For The IoT With Linux
ISBN: 978-1871962611

This is the book that you need to read next if you are using C to write low-level code using small Single Board Computers (SBCs) that run Linux, or if you do any coding in C that interacts with the hardware. As there isn't a good name for this body of knowledge, it isn't easy to find a single source for it. This book gathers together all of these low-level, hardware-oriented and often hardware-specific ideas. As such it is a moderately advanced book. This is not to say that it is difficult, but it does presuppose that you already know how to program in C and that you know the basic idioms of C, which have been covered in this book.

Starting off from the very simple task of making a program run automatically, we look at how your program works with user-mode Linux. If you are working with hardware, arithmetic cannot be ignored. Separate chapters are devoted to integer, fixed-point and floating-point arithmetic. Equally, to handle I/O you need to have a good grasp of files and the pseudo file system - sysfs in particular. The dev/mem file coupled with memory-mapped files makes it possible to work with raw memory without leaving user mode. Sockets are general-purpose way of communicating over networks and similar infrastructure and here the focus is on sending data over the internet and for this we build a web client and a server. Next comes the idea of mutitasking using Pthreads. As well as looking at threads, we consider locking, using mutex and condition variables, and scheduling. Although interrupts don't exist in user-mode Linux, we can get very close using poll and threading. Now that multiple cores are a feature of even low-cost SBC, in later chapters we cover managing cores, look at C11's atomics and introduce its memory models and barriers. Finally we take a short look at how to mix assembler with C.

Raspberry Pi IoT in C
ISBN: 978-1871962468

The Raspberry Pi makes an ideal match for the Internet of Things. To put it to good use in IoT you need two areas of expertise, electronics and programming in the C language and, because of the way hardware and software engineering tend to occupy separate niches, you may need help with combining the two. This book teaches you to think like an IoT programmer. After reading it you will be in a better position to tackle interfacing anything-with-anything without the need for custom drivers and pre-built hardware modules.

If you want to know how to work with the GPIO lines directly, how to work with near realtime Linux, and generally take control of the Pi, this is the book you need. It explains how to use the standard bus types - SPI, I2C, PWM - and with custom protocols including an in-depth exposition of the 1-wire bus. You will also discover how to put the Internet into the IoT using sockets and the low cost ESP8266. Throughout the book takes a practical approach, helping readers to understand electronic circuits and datasheets and translate this to code, specifically using the C programming language.

The main reason for choosing C is speed, a crucial factor when you are writing programs to communicate with the outside world. If you are familiar with another programming language, C shouldn't be hard to pick up. Here it is used in conjunction with NetBeans and with the bcm2835 library.

The main idea in this book is to not simply install a driver, but to work directly with the hardware. So rather than using Raspberry Pi HATs or other expansion boards we use the Pi's GPIO and connect off-the-shelf sensors.

Micro:bit IoT In C
ISBN: 978-1871962451

The BBC micro:bit is capable of taking on a variety of roles including that of a powerful IoT device. In order to gain full access to its features and to external devices, however, you need to use C. which delivers the speed crucial to programs that communicate with the outside world. This book, written for the electronics enthusiast with a programming background, presents details of sensors and circuits with several complete programs.

A first "Hello Blinky" C program introduces the mbed online compiler, after that an offline approach using the yotta development environment plus NetBeans is used to discover how to control the micro:bit's I/O lines and explore the basis of using the GPIO. For speed we need to work directly with the raw hardware and also master memory mapping and pulse width modulation.

Sensors are connected using first the I2C bus, then by implementing a custom protocol for a one-wire bus, and eventually adding eight channels of 12-bit AtoD with the SPI bus, which involves overcoming some subtle difficulties and serial connections. The micro: bit lacks WiFi connectivity but using a low-cost device it can become an Internet server via its serial port.

To conclude we look at the micro:bit's LED display. This may only be 5x5, but it is very versatile, especially when you use pulse width modulation to vary the brightness level, something demonstrated in the classic game Commando Jump, written in C.